BRITAIN AND IRELAND

PEARSON EDUCATION

We work with leading authors to develop the
strongest educational materials in history,
bringing cutting-edge thinking and best learning
practice to a global market.

Under a range of well-known imprints, including
Longman, we craft high quality
print and electronic publications which help
readers to understand and apply their content,
whether studying or at work.

To find out more about the complete range of our
publishing please visit us on the World Wide Web at:
www.pearsoned-ema.com

Britain and Ireland: From Home Rule to Independence

JEREMY SMITH

LONGMAN

An imprint of **PEARSON EDUCATION**

Harlow, England · London · New York · Reading, Massachusetts · San Francisco ·
Toronto · Don Mills, Ontario · Sydney · Tokyo · Singapore · Hong Kong · Seoul ·
Taipei · Cape Town · Madrid · Mexico City · Amsterdam · Munich · Paris · Milan

Pearson Education Limited
Edinburgh Gate
Harlow
Essex CM20 2JE
England

and Associated Companies throughout the world.

Visit us on the World Wide Web at:
www.pearsoned-ema.com

First published 2000

© Pearson Education Limited 1999

The right of Jeremy Smith to be identified as author
of this Work has been asserted by him in accordance
with the Copyright, Designs and Patents Act 1988.

ISBN 0-582-30193-9 PPR

British Library Cataloguing-in-Publication Data
A catalogue record for this book is available from the British Library

Library of Congress Cataloging-in-Publication Data
A catalog record for this book is available from the Library of Congress

Set by 7 in 10/12 Sabon
Printed in Malaysia, VVP

CONTENTS

AN INTRODUCTION TO THE SERIES

Such is the pace of historical enquiry in the modern world that there is an ever-widening gap between the specialist article or monograph, incorporating the results of current research, and general surveys, which inevitably become out of date. *Seminar Studies in History* are designed to bridge this gap. The series was founded by Patrick Richardson in 1966 and his aim was to cover major themes in British, European and World history. Between 1980 and 1996 Roger Lockyer continued his work, before handing the editorship over to Clive Emsley and Gordon Martel. Clive Emsley is Professor of History at the Open University, while Gordon Martel is Professor of International History at the University of Northern British Columbia, Canada and Senior Research Fellow at De Montfort University.

All the books are written by experts in their field who are not only familiar with the latest research but have often contributed to it. They are frequently revised, in order to take account of new information and interpretations. They provide a selection of documents to illustrate major themes and provoke discussion, and also a guide to further reading. The aim of *Seminar Studies* is to clarify complex issues without over-simplifying them, and to stimulate readers into deepening their knowledge and understanding of major themes and topics.

NOTE ON REFERENCING SYSTEM

Readers should note that numbers in square brackets [5] refer them to the corresponding entry in the Bibliography at the end of the book (specific page numbers are given in italics). A number in square brackets preceded by *Doc.* [*Doc. 5*] refers readers to the corresponding item in the Documents section which follows the main text.

PUBLISHER'S ACKNOWLEDGEMENTS

The publishers are grateful to the following for permission to reproduce copyright material:

Penguin UK for an extract from *Paddy and Mr. Punch: Connections in Irish and English History* by R.F. Foster (Viking 1993), copyright © R.F. Foster 1993; Pluto Press for an extract from *Fenianism in Mid-Victorian Britain* by J. Newsinger (1994); the Controller of Her Majesty's Stationery Office, Norwich, for an extract from *Irish Unionism 1885–1923: A Documentary History* by P. Buckland (1973) copyright © Crown copyright, Proni reference number D/989/C/3/5 Deputy Keeper of the Records, Public Record Office of Northern Ireland; Pearse Museum, Dublin, for O'Donovan Rossa's funeral address by Patrick Pearse; Weidenfeld and Nicolson and Michael Collins (nephew) for the funeral address for Thomas Ashe by Michael Collins taken from *Ireland since the Famine* by F.S.L. Lyons (1971); A.P. Watt Ltd on behalf of Michael B. Yeats and Simon & Schuster, Inc. for the poem, 'Easter 1916' from *The Poems of W.B. Yeats: A New Edition* edited by Richard J. Finneran, copyright © 1924 by Macmillan Publishing Company, renewed 1952 by Bertha Georgie Yeats; Colin Smythe Limited for an extract from *The Insurrection in Dublin* by James Stephens (1992).

Whilst every effort has been made to trace the owners of copyright material, in a few cases this has proved impossible and so we take this opportunity to offer our apologies to any copyright holders whose rights we may have unwittingly infringed.

AUTHOR'S ACKNOWLEDGEMENTS

I would like to thank Mr Alan Beattie and Dr Stuart Ball for all their encouragement and advice over a number of years. Dr Roger Lockyer was helpful at an early stage in the venture, while Dr Alvin Jackson was most kind in reading an earlier draft of the text, the final version of which has gained substantially from his expert reflections. At Longman Hilary Shaw has been an invaluable guide into the requirements of a student text. Thanks also to Sarah Bury for struggling heroically with my spelling. Friends at Radley were (and are) a loud and entertaining distraction, in particular the Greeds, the Davenports and the Kings, while the History Department has been a source of support and interest. Charlie and Tigy have been far more than a man's best friends. To Pud I owe everything, not least the arrival of our own little 'big fella', Fred Eifion Smith.

PART ONE: THE BACKGROUND

1 IRISH HISTORY AND THE HISTORIANS

Until the 1950s, the dominant interpretation of nineteenth-century Ireland represented the period as the climax of seven centuries of struggle between an emerging Irish nation and a tyrannical English imperialism [*Doc. 1*]. That struggle, dating from the twelfth century when England began meddling in Irish affairs, was formalised in 1801 with the Act of Union that absorbed Ireland into the United Kingdom. From this point on, Ireland's story was primarily a nationalist struggle to throw off English colonial rule and recover her liberty, and after numerous political campaigns, violent agitations and a war of liberation she finally achieved independence from Britain in 1921. In other words, Ireland's history was a deliverance tale, with the nationalist perspective forming a central spine to any understanding of her past.

From the 1940s onwards, this began to change slowly as historians revised their opinions on many of the key episodes in the nationalist interpretation. In place of a 'Brit-bashing version of history' [190 *p. 2*] they offered alternative understandings, which criticised the traditional view of Irish history and which were, according to them, more balanced, less partisan and more thoroughly researched. So extensive and broad was this questioning of orthodoxies that by the 1980s few of the cherished nationalist verities survived intact. Commentators and historians, particularly those critical of assaults upon the traditional nationalist paradigm, now spoke, rather disparagingly, of a new 'revisionist' interpretation of Irish history and of a fully developed school of 'revisionist' Irish historians [*Doc. 2*].

THE NATIONALIST INTERPRETATION

According to the 'grand nationalist narrative', a distinct Irish people, based upon a distinct Gaelic language and culture, had already long existed before the first of several English invasions from the twelfth century. Over time the native Irish were dispossessed of their historic rights in order to safeguard England's interests. Their land passed into the hands of an English ruling elite and their political rights were subjugated. The Irish Parliament was gradually reduced to subservience under the British Crown, through Poynings' Law in 1494 which made its legislative powers subordinate to the English Privy Council, and later extended with the Declaratory Act of 1720 which reaffirmed British parliamentary supremacy[12; 27]. More significantly, the religious freedom of the Irish was curbed given their sturdy refusal to desert the Catholic Church following the English Reformation in the sixteenth century. Despite attempts to force Protestantism onto Ireland, with the plantation of Scottish Presbyterians into the province of Ulster from 1610 and Cromwell's bloody campaigns and resettlements of the 1650s [34], the majority of Ireland's population kept the Catholic faith. Since England remained resolutely Anglican, it was a situation pregnant with difficulties. These came to a head with the attempt by James II to return England to Rome. Irish support for his venture simply confirmed, for the English, the disloyalty and danger posed to their security by a Catholic Ireland. The subsequent overthrow of James II in 1688 and arrival of the new Protestant King of England, William of Orange, encouraged the English to conclude that if they could not force Ireland into the Anglican Church they could at least marginalise and suppress it as a potential threat. As such, Britain established a Protestant Parliament in Ireland, ruled by a small, landed, non-Catholic elite and buttressed by the Anglican Church of Ireland. This elite, known as the Protestant Ascendancy, now dominated the political and social life of Ireland. Through a series of Penal Laws Catholics lost political rights: from 1728 they were unable to vote, hold office in the army, administration and government, gain employment in the professions, or enter a university. Restrictions on Catholic ownership of land tightened; by 1703 they held just 14 per cent of the land [67; 97]. Thus by the end of the eighteenth century, Ireland was an occupied nation whose land had been stolen, whose political power had been seized and whose religious freedoms had been denied by an alien, English, Anglican ruling ascendancy, backed by the British state. Yet in the breast of every true Irishman and woman (implicitly 'true' meant Catholic) burned the desire to throw out the English and re-take control of their country.

Their opportunity came during the dramatic political events of the 1780s and 1790s. Against a backdrop of revolution in America, calls for greater independence for Ireland came from Volunteer groups, set up in the 1770s to protect Ireland from the enemies of Britain, as well as from the Patriots, a group of landed Protestants inside the Irish

Parliament. Desperately short of money and militarily overstretched, Britain relented to the pressure in 1782 by repealing the Declaratory Act and allowing the Irish Parliament the right to introduce its own laws. This experiment in partial independence, operating under the title of Grattan's Parliament after one of the Patriot leaders, lit the fuse to a much bigger explosion against British control, with the outbreak of rebellion in 1798. It was led by Wolfe Tone and the United Irishmen, who demanded an Irish republic 'to break the connection with England, the never failing source of all our political evils' [27 *p. 15*]. Here, for nationalist historians, were the Irish people at last rising up to throw off their chains and demand their freedom, only to be crushed by the ruthless repression of the British military and to witness the suppression of Grattan's Parliament. Refusing to recognise the veracity of Irish national sentiment, Britain now forcibly assimilated Ireland into her political structure with the Act of Union. Union provided the clearest example of English imperialism, the sacrifice of Ireland's national destiny at the altar of England's strategic, political and economic interests.

Resistance to British rule, though crushed, was not forgotten by the Catholic majority. Instead it was re-directed, by the 1820s, into more constitutional channels under the leadership of an Irish lawyer, Daniel O'Connell. His movement to emancipate Catholics from their legal discrimination mobilised much of Ireland behind him and was followed in the 1830s and 1840s by an unsuccessful campaign to repeal the Act of Union itself. National sentiment also flowed behind the Young Ireland movement, a group of enthusiasts who pursued a cultural and literary path to independence by reviving ancient Gaelic 'myths' and stories. Meanwhile the Fenians, a political group named after ancient Irish warriors, maintained Tone's commitment to violent revolution as the only true path to Irish liberation. In addition to demanding independence, Nationalists laid the economic problems of mid-nineteenth-century Ireland at the feet of the English. The tragedy of the Great Famine (1845–51), in which over a million Irish people died, was caused by English maladministration and rigid commitment to the 'laws' of political economy; many even assumed it was manufactured by the English to teach the Irish a lesson and dampen their national sentiment. It was also a sign of Ireland's failure to join in the modernisation process that was transforming society on the British mainland, the cause of which again lay with English mismanagement. Similarly, problems with the land, and particularly the habitual tensions between tenants and landlords, were part of a wider struggle between the dispossessed 'Irish' farmers and an English, Anglican landowning class. Indeed the cause of Ireland's rural impoverishment, her economic backwardness and her agricultural depression lay firmly with the evils of landlordism, which extracted wealth to London, evicted tenants at will and exercised a brutal, harsh regime across the Irish countryside. If Union provided the framework for English oppression, then the landlords were the shock-troops of English imperialism. For historians, the struggle for the land was part of a larger struggle for Ireland.

Indeed it was the struggle over the land that re-energised the nationalist movement, sleeping since the collapse of O'Connell's repeal campaign but now under the inspiring leadership of Charles Stewart Parnell. By the early 1880s, Parnell repaired and strengthened the nationalist organisation, enabling it to win mass support across Ireland, except in Ulster, and force a British government to offer them Home Rule in 1886. Again, however, Ireland's national destiny was betrayed by the English, who orchestrated an alliance of Irish landlords and Ulster Protestants, alongside the wider British Establishment, in order to defeat Home Rule. Without leadership, following Parnell's untimely death in 1891, the nationalist movement declined and Ireland returned to a state of brooding resignation. National enthusiasm flowed into cultural spheres, reviving the Gaelic language and Gaelic sports. Some, notably the Fenians, kept the 'physical-force' tradition alive with a belief that only violent insurrection would rid Ireland of England. But their 'self-evident prescience' was out of tune with the general apathy of the period, forcing upon them a lonely if principled wait on the margins of Irish politics, for their call to come in the future.

That moment finally arrived at Easter 1916 when a small band of Irish nationalists, led by Patrick Pearse and James Connolly, rose in rebellion and took on the might of the British Empire. Though defeated and subsequently executed, the men of 1916 re-ignited the nationalist cause in Ireland and rallied the Irish people against English rule. Under the leadership of Eamon de Valera and his Sinn Féin party, a united Irish nation now rejected colonial rule and pressed for independence, only to be met by yet more brutal oppression from the British government. This time the Irish did not buckle under the weight of English coercion but engaged in a war of national liberation between 1919 and 1921. Britain threw all she had against them, endorsing murderous methods that recalled the worst excesses of Cromwell, but was unable to defeat the massed Irish nation and particularly its military forces, the Irish Republican Army (IRA). Exhausted and nearly bankrupt, the British government at last gave way in 1921 and granted Dominion status to Ireland. Seven centuries of colonial domination came to an end.

In other words, what we might term the orthodox nationalist interpretation offered a version of Ireland's past as one of 'an unbroken tradition of resistance to British rule' [52 *p. 107*], a thread or paradigm that was central to any understanding of nineteenth-century Ireland [*Doc. 1*]. The strength and survival of this interpretation owed much to its usefulness. It furnished the newly created Irish nation-state with a sympathetic 'past', a history that supplied a sense of purpose and direction, so establishing an uninterrupted connection between where the nation had come from, where it was, and where it was going. Such a connection gave Ireland an ancestry or 'bloodline', equipping its new political leaders with the legitimacy and authority to rule over the Irish people [49]. Having a common national inheritance gave cohesion and unity to Irish society (except for Protestants in Ulster, who created their own cultural inheritance), regardless of their different regional or class identities and their deep political divisions following the civil war of 1922–23. It gave Ireland a shared set of values and beliefs. Society now looked to the self-sacrifice and dedication of Wolfe Tone or the 1916 'martyrs' for moral guidance, evolving what Boyce calls 'public morality tales' [39 *p. 1*]. The bravery of Ireland's national leaders, be they Tone, Parnell or Michael Collins, leader of the IRA, were used to inspire and instruct the young, their deeds glorified as an example to others. Moreover, the maintenance of the nationalist interpretation owed a great deal to the survival of those political leaders brought to power in 1921: it is instructive to remember that de Valera, one of the leaders of the 1916 Rising, was President of the Irish Republic until 1973. It was also a representation sustained by deep institutional conservatism within Irish society, in the media, the Church, local government and most importantly in the education system [43].

THE RISE OF 'REVISIONISM'

From the 1940s challenges to the orthodox nationalist interpretation began to appear. A small group of historians, notably R.D. Edwards and T. Moody, set themselves the task of revealing the 'true' Irish past by questioning the prevailing 'nationalist myths' that dominated academic and popular understandings of Ireland's history [46]. Through rigorous empirical research and objective professionalism, and associated with a new journal *Irish Historical Studies* founded in 1938, they offered alternative perspectives on Ireland's story. New ideas and views appeared across the whole period of Anglo–Irish affairs: indeed some of the earliest reinterpretations were on Ireland under the Tudors. For the nineteenth century, this early 'revisionist' impulse focused on the dominating issues of the Great Famine and the land question. The Irish Famine, for example, slowly took on a new appearance as less a catastrophe precipitated by English connivance than one caused by endemic weakness and structural limitations in the Irish economy; British policy was characterised more by muddle and well-intentioned ineptitude than by conscious design [72]. Similarly, problems with the land were no longer laid solely at the feet of a grasping, oppressive, alien landlord class, a characterisation increasingly seen as a fiction. What began to emerge was a more balanced picture: a landlord class less inclined to evict a tenant on a 'whim' than to try and reach a compromise or even forgo rent during particularly hard periods; a class less distinct from its surrounding tenantry, in both religious and cultural terms; a class still motivated by older paternalistic concerns, despite being under severe economic strain.

More generally, the nature of Irish politics during the nineteenth century began to alter. Instead of witnessing the inexorable growth of a national liberationist movement in a linear trajectory from Tone to O'Connell to Parnell, and on to Pearse by 1916, a much more complex development was unfolding. It was typified as much by cooperation and co-existence between landlords and tenants or Protestants and Catholics, as by conflict. Nationalist forces suffered retreat, disappointment and division alongside steady advance. And people's concerns orientated towards everyday, local matters, such as grazing rights, family feuds, employment, rent levels, religious disputes, land squabbles, food prices, local patronage and deference, as much as they did to more altruistic questions of national self-determination [81].

By the 1970s, Ireland's history looked very different. Fresh and often critical perspectives on most of the key episodes of the nationalist interpretation had been presented. Such perspectives, labelled 'revisionist' by nationalist critics, tended to be sceptical of orthodox explanations, less judgemental and more sensitive to the precise nature of Britain's involvement in Ireland or the activities of Irish landlords. They were intrigued by other traditions within Irish society, such as Unionism, and interested in the diversity of Irish experiences, concerned to challenge widely held and popular assumptions, as well as branch out into new areas [*Doc. 2*]. For example, through two new journals, *Irish Economic and Social History* and *Saothar*, Ireland's economy under the Union was analysed using economic statistics and theory rather than established preconceptions. Cultural developments at the end of the nineteenth century were investigated. Irish Unionism received its first major study in 1972 [111; 112]. Heroes of the nationalist pantheon were reassessed in terms far from flattering to the nationalist cause. Parnell, for example, emerged as a rather conservative politician, more at home in London than Ireland. De Valera resembled a rather devious figure, obsessed with his position at the head of the nationalist movement. And Patrick Pearse appeared in Ruth Dudley Edwards's study as a curious, remote and somewhat 'unhealthy' individual [263]. Little was spared. Even the 'foundation moment' of modern Ireland, the Easter Rising of 1916 when the Irish nation rose from its sleep, was re-evaluated as a confused, incompetent and unpopular event, led by an undemocratic group of dreamers. So shocking was this particular reassessment, written at the time of the 50th anniversary of the Rising by Father Francis Shaw, that its publication was suspended for several years. The volume of research brought about a softening in the orthodox nationalist interpretation, a broader understanding of Ireland's past, a greater recognition of mistakes and limitations, and a willingness to criticise as well as idolise heroes. All these reservations were reflected in one of the finest expositions of modern Irish history, F.S.L. Lyons's *Ireland Since the Famine*, published in 1971. But this did not stop the overall speed and direction of the 'revisionist' bandwagon. By 1980 the assault was sufficiently established to warrant its canonisation into the *New History of Ireland* series, and its popularisation by Roy Foster in his *Modern Ireland, 1600–1972*.

For some it seemed, that by the 1980s, 'revisionism' had become the new orthodoxy for understanding Ireland's past, and this in turn drew a bitter response from the nationalist community. In 1989 Brendan Bradshaw published a now seminal article, ironically in *Irish Historical Studies*, criticising revisionist history for what he saw as its ill-disguised hostility to the nationalist interpretation of Ireland's history [40]. His attack centred on revisionism's removal of all the human experience and pain from what was, by any standards, a tragic past, and offering in its place a sanitised and value-free version that 'filtered out the trauma', so creating a wholly misleading account [42 *p. 196*]. This was a vital omission since the modern community of Ireland was now denied its history, a connection to 'its' past with the historian duty-bound to bridge that past to the present: of course one might ask which past and indeed which present were being connected [44]. Bradshaw went further, attacking revisionists for their inflated claims to be objective and dispassionate in their account. On the contrary, their understandings of Irish history were just as biased as the nationalist one, for attempts to write neutral history simply foundered on the historian's inevitably subjective input. In fact, their pretensions to objectivity hid, more sinisterly, a pro-British or soft-Unionist outlook, or, for others like Seamus Deane, were the product of late-twentieth-century economic development and the rise of new consumer values, an environment where Ireland's national story had no place or role [177].

In many respects Bradshaw intellectualised what was felt within wider public opinion in Ireland and America. For beyond the ivory towers of academia, many of which were now firmly planted in England, popular understandings of Irish history stuck more or less to the orthodox nationalist version of events. Declan Kiberd pointed to a poll by the *Irish Independent* newspaper in 1991, at the time of the 75th anniversary of the Easter Rising, in which 58 per cent of those asked thought the rebels were right to take up arms, while 65 per cent still looked on the event with pride [190]. In addition, some of the most recent work has injected new life into the nationalist account. Studies by Cairns and Richards, in *Writing Ireland* [286], and Declan Kiberd's *Inventing Ireland* [300], in applying post-colonial ideas to Ireland, have offered a more complex and intriguing account of the rise of Irish nationalist identities defined by and against English imperialism [303].

Of course the ongoing debate between nationalist orthodoxy and the so-called 'revisionist' school sets up a false dichotomy. For what has actually been taking place is a closer and more detailed scrutiny of documentary sources (much of which was not available to previous historians) and the application of new theories to research. Historiography since the 1940s is better viewed as a broadening of our knowledge on Ireland's past rather than a revision of it. All history writing after all is an unceasing process of change, challenge and response. And in this sense Foster's claim that 'we are all revisionists now' is hard to dispute [47]. Far from representing a conspiratorial clique dedicated to an anti-national project, 'Irish historians have done nothing remarkable by the standards of their profession. They have simply applied, in the Irish context, the same approaches and methods as are taken for granted by their counterparts in other countries' [52 *p. 114*]. Current trends in research on Irish history seem to reflect this by appearing little affected by the political-centred, revisionist/nationalist debate. For example, the expansion of women's and feminist history [293; 305] over recent years has deepened our knowledge of this much-neglected area. Studies of the Irish heritage industry [284] or research into definitions of Ireland and Irishness (place and identity) have also grown steadily, as with a collection of essays edited by B. Graham entitled *In Search of Ireland* [297]. Popular Irish culture is another growth industry, once associated with specialist journals such as *Irish Studies Review, Eire-Ireland* and various Field Day publications, but now entering more mainstream studies [294]. What is clear, then, is that our present vision and understanding of Ireland's past is much more sophisticated and nuanced than 40, or even 20 years ago. Hence the need for a new *Seminar Study* on the subject to replace Grenfell Morton's excellent study published in 1980.

IRELAND'S PAST, 1800–69

BINDING IRELAND, 1800–22

On 1 January 1801, the Act of Union absorbed Ireland into the British Constitution, forming the United Kingdom of Great Britain and Ireland. At a stroke it abolished the Irish Parliament that had sat at College Green for several centuries and had operated relatively independently of Westminster since 1782, following repeal of the Declaratory Act and the Renunciation Act of 1783. Abolition of Grattan's Parliament (1782–1800), so-called after the Irish leader who had done most to win it, led to the transference of 100 Irish MPs and 28 Peers (plus four spiritual Peers) to the Imperial Parliament at Westminster. The Churches of Ireland and England were joined, guaranteeing the property, tithe and supremacy of the Anglican Church in Ireland. Clearly, then, Union heralded significant change to Ireland's political structure. But some continuity was also evident. For example, the Crown remained sovereign over all Irish territory, as it had been since 1541 when Henry VIII took the title King of Ireland [21]. Ireland's legal system, army establishment and system of landholding were all maintained and the direction of Irish affairs remained the charge of the Lord Lieutenant and Chief Secretary, at the head of an administration based at Dublin Castle. This mixture of change and continuity meant Ireland's 'Union was incomplete' [106 p. 37] and fell some way short of full absorbtion, occupying a unique position within the British Empire. Of course incompleteness of Union and the points of continuity in areas such as law and civil administration perpetuated a sense of Irish separateness amongst certain groups, particularly the Protestant patriots like Grattan. And in reminding the Irish 'that there once had been an Irish Parliament' [106 p. 34], it left open the possibility that there could be one again.

At one level, the Act of Union was part of the centralising tendency of British government during the late eighteenth century under the direction of William Pitt, the Prime Minister (1783–1801). More immediately it was a response to the outbreak of rebellion in Ireland in 1798, led by the republican Wolfe Tone and the radical association of the United Irishmen. The revolt was sparked by the impact of new revolutionary ideas coming from America and France, and the economic pressures of war between Britain and France, since 1793. It began as a strike against continued British involvement in Ireland, looking to France for aid and drawing support from both Catholics and Dissenters in Ulster. However, its non-denominational basis did not survive as religious differences increasingly spilled over into sectarian violence and were accompanied by agrarian unrest, with attacks upon landlords. Sectarian divisions and the limited geographic spread of resistance enabled Britain to crush the rebellion quickly, though leaving Pitt convinced that British security was compromised by Ireland. His remedy was to subsume her into the British polity with a plan for legislative union. It met with strong resistance from within the Irish Parliament, led by the Patriots Henry Grattan, John Foster and John Curran, and from Dissenters in Ulster who feared a British Parliament would show too much leniency to Catholics. Yet with much bribery and a liberal promising of offices and peerages, much of it the work of Lord Castlereagh the Irish Chief Secretary, Pitt was able to steer the measure successfully through the Irish Parliament and then the British one. Union was therefore born of a short-term emergency, but it also sought long-term solutions to problems that had endlessly bedevilled Britain. It gave protection to British trading and commercial interests in America and the West Indies. It shored-up western defences after an attempted French landing in 1796–97 and again at Killala Bay in September 1798, and was part of a wider move to restructure and strengthen the British Empire. In this sense the Act of Union must be placed alongside the India Act of 1784 and Canada Act of 1791, which shared the common objective of forestalling another imperial catastrophe like that of 1776–82, when America was lost [61].

Of course our knowledge that the Union was finally abandoned in 1921 might easily suggest that the British were, during the years that followed its inception in 1801, in a state of hopeless and inevitable retreat. Such a representation was by no means obvious to the British, who set about crafting Ireland into a contented member of the United Kingdom, in a similar fashion to Scotland after its Union in 1707. Ireland's economy was integrated slowly into the British economy, with fusion of the taxation system and exchequer by 1817. Customs and tariffs were harmonised, with a free trade area for the entire British Isles operative from 1825 [84]. Britain also practised what might be termed cultural imperialism. With Union came the spread of British customs, beliefs, games and sports, and most significantly written and spoken English. This became the medium of government, law, trade, newspapers, books, road signs and over time the idiom of the ordinary people, particularly with the creation of a national system of elementary education in 1831. The imposition of English customs and language encouraged the Irish to be reconstructed as British, what Declan Kiberd refers to as 'the creation of a secret England called Ireland' [300 *p. 15*], and thus into a contented and disciplined part of the UK. In this sense, Britain justified its project in Ireland not as an act of conquest but as a moral crusade [286] bringing civilisation, reason and progress to an Irish people long seen by popular stereotype as 'lazy, dirty, improvident, irresolute, feckless, made menacing by their numbers and by their dotish allegiance to a sinister and subversive religion' [192 *p. 4*].

British rule was also assisted by support from important groups within the native Irish population. The most receptive were the Protestant landed elites, who had dominated Irish affairs since 1688 and were able to command great social influence and economic power. Their earlier hostility towards legislative union, as witnessed in the Irish Parliament, quickly disappeared as its benefits became clear [16]. It offered security for their property and for their Church against the Catholic majority, opportunities for social and political advancement amongst the metropolitan elite in London, and generous access to offices and patronage at court. Within a generation the Protestant Ascendancy elites had re-invented themselves as loyal defenders of the Union. Similarly, the once suspicious Presbyterian Dissenters of Ulster also recognised the advantage of Union with Britain, as a source of protection against Catholics, in a sort of Anglo-Irish pan-Protestant alliance.

THREATS TO THE UNION, 1823–44

British rule did encounter problems. Most immediately threatening was the spread of rural violence during the early 1800s. Agrarian agitation was a traditional, almost endemic, feature of Irish society, aimed against a harsh landlord or high food prices or exorbitant tithes [63; 68]. Often the agitation was channelled through secret, oath-bound societies that took exotic names such as the Rapparees, Levellers, Oakboys, Steelers, Houghers, Strawboys and Whiteboys, and were led by a local 'big man' or captain with a similarly colourful pseudonym, often reflecting his particular talent: Slasher, Lightfoot,

Cropper, Echo, Fearnot, Burnstack [86; 107]. The societies upheld a sort of communal moral code of conduct. Breaking that code, be it by raising rents, an unfair eviction, theft or a land dispute, could result in rough, sometimes violent, justice against the person accused, such as beatings, cutting off ears or even murder, or against their property, such as the maiming of cattle, destroying walls and fences, or burning homes. It is important to stress that conflict did not always result from simple landlord versus tenant farmer antagonisms, but as often would involve labourers against tenant farmers or one neighbour against another or one village against another or even a family feud. The period 1813–18, and again in 1829–33, witnessed a revival of agricultural violence, under the label of Whiteboyism, across west and central Ireland. In this case the unrest was the result of a collapse in agricultural prices after 1815 and the gradual shift from arable to livestock farming, with the spread of grazing, which fuelled rural unemployment. It also occurred against a backdrop of rapid population growth that helped reduce wage levels, raised food prices and forced families to subdivide their land into uneconomic plots, so creating intense pressure on landholding [96; 104; 105; 108]. Agrarian unrest stretched Britain's ability to maintain law and order, forcing the government into a series of *ad hoc* initiatives [69]. In 1814 the Chief Secretary, Sir Robert Peel, introduced stipendiary magistrates and the Peace Preservation Corps to beef up the forces of coercion, which in 1822 were supplemented by a County Constabulary. In 1836 these organisations were consolidated into the Irish Constabulary, on the initiative of the reform-minded Thomas Drummond, Under-Secretary at the Irish Office from 1835 to 1840.

However, the greatest danger to the Union was the rise of a popular movement dedicated to removing discrimination against Catholics, particularly their bar from sitting in Parliament, even though they could vote if they met the requisite property qualification [97]. Emancipation was promised to Catholics by Pitt as part of the Act of Union, only to be vetoed by King George III, so forcing Pitt's resignation from office. This was a serious mistake, for many Catholics actually welcomed Union with Britain, believing government from Westminster would be more equitable to their interests. Westminster had already exercised its influence over the Irish Protestant Parliament by forcing through Catholic relief measures, as with the 1778 Act allowing Catholics to own land and in 1782 an Act removing restraints on their education. In addition the Catholic Church shared Pitt's opposition to the godless republican ideas of the United Irishmen and his concern for maintaining the existing social order. Failure to introduce political emancipation for Catholics prevented British rule from firmly anchoring itself within Irish society or from gaining the sponsorship of perhaps the most powerful influence over the majority of Ireland's population, the Catholic Church. And by denying Catholics a place within the British Constitution, they helped define 'Britishness' as an exclusively Protestant identity, in conflict with a Catholic 'Other' [64]. As a result, whereas in Scotland Britishness fostered unity and obscured differences with the English, thus stabilising their Union, in Ireland Britishness merely acted to divide and distinguish the majority of Irish people from the English, so obstructing stability.

It was Daniel O'Connell, a Catholic lawyer, who transformed Catholic resentment over the emancipation issue into a nationwide campaign, under the control of the Catholic Association which he formed in 1823 [98; 280]. The Association was dedicated to forcing the emancipation of Catholics onto the British government under pressure from a mass campaign. Through the power of his own rhetoric, a sympathetic local clergy and above all a small 'rent' paid to the Association outside each local church, O'Connell mobilised a popular movement composed of Catholics from all manner of backgrounds: middle-class individuals such as farmers, shopkeepers, publicans, as well as labourers and cottiers. The movement grew quickly and acquired a broader appeal as champion of Catholic interests, defender of their rights and even a little later the liberator of what many Catholics imagined was their dispossessed nation. Catholicism and nationalism began to combine under the Association.

Of course the problem still remained of pressuring the British government into granting emancipation. O'Connell was a master of tactics and looked to influence the outcome of by-elections, having witnessed the pro-emancipation Henry Villiers Stuart elected for Waterford in 1826 with local Association help. O'Connell himself now stood at Clare in 1828 and won. This demonstration of the popular 'platform' politics posed immense dangers to Protestant landownership and to the government's authority in Ireland: O'Connell, it seemed, had a movement far bigger than the forces of law and order and one capable of dominating the political fortunes of much of Ireland. In these circumstances for the government simply to nullify the Clare vote would have provoked serious disturbances if not civil war. The only alternative which the Tory government, led by the Duke of Wellington and Peel, took was to grant emancipation in 1829 [101].

The decision rested on Wellington and Peel's belief that the maintenance of governmental authority now necessitated emancipation, whereas a year earlier it had required resistance. In addition, they believed it would open up a new chapter in Anglo–Irish relations, leading to better social and sectarian relations from which stability and prosperity would develop, and weld Catholics into loyal supporters of British rule. Of course the downside for them was that it destroyed the unity of the Tory party, which fell from power a year hence, and irreparably damaged the Protestant Ascendancy's domination of Irish society. Irish Protestants regarded it as a sell-out, and the Act of Union no longer a fixed settlement but forever at the mercy of party politics and public opinion. It fed a revival of militant Protestantism, through the Orange Order and new Brunswick clubs, much of which was centred in Ulster, as well as the spread of Evangelical Anglican missions throughout Ireland, to wean ordinary Irish folk from what the missions argued was a superstitious, oppressive and irrational Catholic Church. All these different movements gave an added sharpness to sectarian tensions during the 1830s and 1840s.

O'Connell was now at the apogee of his career. He had mobilised a popular Liberal–nationalist movement that had extracted far-reaching changes from a British government, something which the Liberal political movements of Europe singularly failed to achieve throughout the 1830s and 1840s. In this he had shown Westminster as an arena where the Irish could do business, and between 1830 and 1841, with his band of 40-odd MPs elected at the 1832 election, he played the party political game with skill and relish [126; 142]. In alliance with the Whig governments (1830–41) and channelling the social discontent of the tithe war in Ireland behind his movement, he pursued and won further reforms [74]. The Irish Church Temporalities Act of 1833 streamlined the Church of Ireland, the Irish Tithe Composition Act of 1832 and the more extensive Tithe Rent-Charge Act of 1838 converted the tithe into a rent charge, paid by the landowner, and in 1838 the Irish Poor Law was introduced. Lastly, in 1840 the Municipal Reform Act established town councils and facilitated the election of O'Connell as the first Catholic mayor of Dublin. Cooperation with the Whig governments of the 1830s had been productive, and was even formalised into a parliamentary compact, the Litchfield House agreement of 1835 [142].

But by the late 1830s, with the imminent demise of the Whig ministry and approach of a Tory government under Peel, O'Connell was compelled towards the larger goal of repealing the Union, launching in April 1840 the Loyal National Repeal Association [90]. This never achieved the success or unity of his emancipation campaign. The Irish electorate remained small and very difficult to mobilise, given confusions with the franchise and the strength of existing political loyalties [25 *p. 21*]. Repeal did not arouse the same degree of enthusiasm and suffered from divisions caused by religious differences and people's concern with local and more immediate issues of life and death. The movement also met head-on a resolute Prime Minister, whose concern for social order had persuaded him to emancipate the Catholics in 1829, but now directed him towards tough, repressive measures. O'Connell's very public retreat from a monster meeting at Clontarf in 1843, after Peel banned it, broke the back of O'Connell's repeal movement. Irish nationalists could stand anything except submission to a British government. O'Connell was himself imprisoned for several months before the decision was reversed by the House of Lords. But far from energising a flagging nationalist career, as it would Parnell, prison 'drained O'Connell's nerve power' [100; 280]. Now 70, he retired from politics.

WHOSE NATION?

The demand for repeal of the Union raised important questions that divided nationalists. What should the Union be replaced with and how would this be achieved? And more contentiously, which groups in Irish society 'rightfully' constituted the Irish nation? For example, literally speaking repeal of the Act of Union could mean the restoration of Grattan's Parliament, an elite Protestant body that denied Catholics their political rights, something O'Connell clearly did not intend. Others thought in terms of a local assembly with charge of day-to-day management of Ireland but still under the sovereignty of the British Crown and part of the British Empire. More extreme enthusiasts hankered after a fully independent Irish republic and were prepared to use violence to achieve it, sections that would later move into the Fenian organisation. O'Connell, though wedded to change through constitutional channels, was himself plagued by uncertainty as to what repeal meant and rarely outlined his thoughts. They almost certainly included a role for the landowning class and some form of connection with Britain, perhaps along federal lines as had been legislated for Canada in 1840; his was after all a 'Loyal' association [59]. Federalism involved the transfer of specific government responsibilities, such as education, health, economic policy, to national assemblies in Ireland, Scotland, Wales and England, while the Westminster Parliament concentrated upon imperial and foreign policy concerns. However, O'Connell never clearly developed these ideas and in public addresses remained vague on details, as much because to have outlined a clear scheme would most likely have divided the nationalist movement.

Confusion existed not only with what should replace the Union, but also which social groups would make up the new Ireland: who, in other words, were the true Irish and who were not. O'Connell's emancipation campaign of the 1820s had made the connection between Catholicism and nationalism, with the struggle for Catholic rights and liberties increasingly coterminous with the struggle for Ireland's rights and freedom [59]. From this it was but a small step to demand restoration of Ireland's freedoms by repealing the Union. Implicit here was an assumption that Irish nationalism correlated with Irish Catholicism and excluded Protestants, landowners and Presbyterian Dissenters in Ulster.

Alternatively, another influential nationalist group, the Young Ireland movement led by Thomas Davies and John Mitchel, was dismayed at the exclusively Catholic basis to O'Connell's nationalism [59; 73]. In its place they advocated a nationalism that transcended Ireland's religious and social differences by uniting all the people on the island of Ireland around a common Irish culture, language and history [286]. Their brand of nationalism was of a broader, more inclusive variety, joining Catholic with Protestant, landlord with tenant, against a common English foe. Through their newspaper, *The Nation*, they sought to win the hearts and minds of their fellow countrymen by espousing a shared history of Ireland, full of Saxon atrocity and English usurpation, a history around which all might unite. A more extreme section of the Young Ireland movement similarly believed sectarian and class differences were of little importance in comparison with the winning of an Irish republic [93]. Commitment to a republic took precedence over a person's background or faith, indeed for some their faith was a republic, venerating the rebellion of 1798 as a sort of 'second coming' and recommending the shedding of blood to achieve it.

Another strain of Irish nationalism to emerge, and similarly hostile to O'Connell's Catholic movement with its democratic undertones, was a form of Protestant patriotism [59; 103]. Composed largely of wealthy landowners and a number of Irish Tories, some 40 of whom were elected to Parliament in 1841, they traced their ancestry back to the independent spirit that infused Grattan and Flood's Patriot group, who resisted Union in 1799. Many of them now advocated a return to the type of partial independence Ireland had enjoyed under Grattan between 1782 and 1800. Their vision for Ireland was one where sectarian divisions were diminished by rule from an impartial, landed elite, whose experience and wealth uniquely equipped them to hold the ring between Ireland's religious groups. Of course critics argued that perhaps they were not all that impartial, given that the majority of land and wealth lay in Protestant hands, and that it was a patriotism born of a fear of democracy and the threat it posed to their property. Despite this, they enjoyed links with the *Freeman's Journal* and their ideas provided the soil from where the Home Government Association would emerge by 1870. By the mid-1840s, Irish nationalism had developed into a broad Church, divided over what type of 'imagined' Irish community to construct and how it was to be built. Yet at moments it could be a mobilising ideology of enormous impact and strength.

No one felt this more than the British administration. Since 1801 it had looked to the Protestant Ascendancy for collaboration in running Ireland. Catholic emancipation, in challenging the authority of British government in Ireland, showed this as untenable. So from 1830 government increasingly pursued a more impartial line, holding the balance between the various religious and social groups within Irish society. This necessitated the reform of outstanding Catholic grievances in order to appease the Catholic middle class and win them over to support for the Union, a policy Boyce calls 'soothing syrup and sugar plums' [16 *p. 96*]. Under Lord Mulgrave, Lord Lieutenant of Ireland, and his able Under-Secretary, Thomas Drummond, the Irish Coercion Act was allowed to expire, Catholics were given political office and received patronage from Dublin Castle. An Irish Poor Law was introduced in 1838 and changes to municipal government and the Irish Church were brought forward.

Peel's ministry (1841–46) followed a similar course, though facing the added pressure of O'Connell's repeal campaign and widespread non–payment of the tithe [90]. These were assaults on the very legitimacy of British government that could not go unchecked. Peel strengthened the legal arm of Dublin Castle and pressed its implementation on a sometimes hesitant magistracy. More dramatically he confronted O'Connell, banning his Clontarf meeting and pressing for his prosecution. For Peel, the Union with Britain would be upheld and defended. But it would also be made more relevant to the needs of the majority of Ireland's population. Peel introduced a Charitable Bequests Bill to manage donations to the Church and granted £100,000 for the establishment of Queen's Colleges in Galway, Belfast and Cork. More damagingly, in terms of his relations to the Tory party, he increased the annual state grant to the Maynooth Catholic seminary in 1845 to £20,000, hoping to encourage a more sympathetic priesthood [85]. He also appointed the Devon Commission in 1843 to investigate landholding and rural impoverishment, to provide the hard facts for future changes. Peel's reforms were a brave effort to tether significant, mostly Catholic, institutions and groups to the Union, so as to stabilise and legitimate British rule with Ireland's population.

In this Peel achieved only limited success. Conciliation certainly won the sympathy of some, but was quickly squandered by his recourse to coercion; the one undermining the other, in a way that would be repeated time and again in Ireland. His reforms upset Irish Protestants, particularly Irish Tories, for pandering to the enemies of Union, while ironically arousing the anger of O'Connell and many in the Catholic hierarchy for threatening their basis of support and power. Reform to improve the status of one section of Irish society simply aroused the wrath of other sections. The concept of 'holding the ring' between Ireland's different social and religious groups was a difficult, if not impossible manoeuvre to effect. Inactivity, for future British administrations in Ireland, looked a far safer and far more realistic assessment of the Irish political landscape

FAMINE AND FENIANS

The whirlwind of the Great Famine that swept across Ireland in 1845–51 proved, for nationalists, the validity of this conclusion. An agricultural society balanced precariously upon a single subsistence crop, with poor communications that were unable to offset the huge regional variations and with a rapidly growing population which increasingly subdivided tenancies into uneconomic units, was a system always vulnerable to crisis. This was seen during the famine of 1816–17. If that society also lacked a cushion of established local employment opportunities or large-scale investment into her economy, thus denying people an alternative source of income, then crisis could easily turn to catastrophe, as happened when the staple food of the populace, the potato, failed three years running [71; 95; 96]. Between 1845 and 1848 nearly a million people died, almost one-tenth of the entire population, and another million were forced to emigrate to the USA. Hardest hit were the labouring and cottier classes of the rural west, but towns also suffered where disease spread fast.

Government measures were not inconsiderable. Price controls were introduced and over £7 million was advanced to purchase Indian meal, establish food depots, soup kitchens and public works (by 1847 750,000 were employed under it), and relieve over-burdened workhouses. These efforts suggest the overall thrust of government policy swept aside its rigid adherence to *laissez-faire* ideas, although its actions were supplemented by private initiative and charities [57; 80]. Even with outside help, the scale and duration of the tragedy simply overwhelmed Dublin Castle; it was a Malthusian nightmare of epic proportions. Nationalists chose not to see these structural and climatic limitations, preferring to interpret the crisis as, at best, the moral bankruptcy and inefficiency of Union, at worst a 'British-generated holocaust' [16 *p. 114*]. For them, responsibility lay squarely with the government's decision not to stop ports from exporting food to wealthier markets or to provide anything like sufficient relief. The latter was a consequence of a misplaced dread of all state intervention and a scarely veiled conviction that the crisis was divine retribution for Irish immorality and fecklessness, typified by Sir Charles Trevelyan, permanent head of the Treasury. At a broader level the dominance of British manufacturing and failure to protect fledgling Irish industries, a consequence of Union, undercut the development of commercial enterprises that might have provided an economic cushion for the Irish people. Young Irelanders, such as John Mitchel and Gavan Duffy, took up these arguments and constructed the Great Famine into what Mary Daly has described as 'another episode in the long-running saga of British mistreatment of Ireland: a nineteenth-century equivalent of the Cromwellian Plantation or the Penal Laws' [72 *p. 73*]. Whatever the actual causes of the enormous tragedy, it quickly became a central feature in the operational mythologies of Irish nationalism.

Yet this was far from evident during the 1850s as people's priorities returned to 'the local, the immediate, and the everyday' [25 *p. 111*], especially towards the traditional institutions and influences in their life. Following a disaster of almost biblical proportions it was no surprise that popular aspirations turned towards the Churches. Both the Catholic and Protestant faiths underwent a devotional revolution during the 1850s and 1860s. In Ulster Presbyterianism grew quickly, providing the cultural bedrock from which a distinct 'Ulster' identity would later emerge. Elsewhere Catholicism strengthened, becoming more assertive in its political role. Under the guidance of Archbishop Cullen [34 *pp. 117–66*] and a Catholic Defence Association, the Church looked to sway Whig/Liberal governments of the mid-nineteenth century into further relief for Catholic grievances, particularly the advancement of denominational education. In 1864 the Catholic-based National Association was formed to continue the fight for educational reform as well as the disestablishment of the Anglican Church of Ireland.

Another traditional aspect of Irish society to revive over the 1850s was the influence of landlords. Famine, ironically, strengthened the position of landlords. Incomes from land rose steadily thanks to a shift from arable to pasture, helped by rising prices on the world market and the easing of pressure to subdivide tenancies, given the fall in Ireland's population. The Encumbered Estates Act (1849) simplified the purchase of bankrupt estates, encouraging the entry of 'new' money, much of it from Catholics, who brought with them ideas for the efficient management of estates [60]. The strengthening of landlord influence enabled them to recover their political power. As O'Connellite repeal politics disintegrated, during the 1850s, Irish politics were dominated by Tories and Liberals, the former winning no less than 55 out of a possible 105 seats at the 1859 election. It appeared, therefore, that whereas the Famine had brought a demographic revolution to Ireland, its political impact was rather minimal. This is not to argue that little was occurring in Ireland between the Famine and the land war of 1879, 'an inherently triumphant Sleeping Beauty laid out on the refrigerated slab of colonial oppression to await the inevitable kiss of some ardent prince' [25 *p. 110*]. Significant pressures developed within Irish society and politics that would shape the direction and tone of Anglo-Irish relations.

The most significant of these pressures concerned problems arising from the land, perhaps inevitably so after the Famine. These were broad and varied, often cutting across class, region and religious boundaries, although by the 1850s they concentrated upon the rivalry between tenant farmers and landowners [104; 105]. Tenant farmers were increasingly assertive from the acquisition of the franchise in 1850, from rising expectations born of increases in the price of food and from continued emigration that eased competition for landholdings. Rivalry between farmers and landlords was based upon traditional irritants of rent, tenure and the compensation for improvements, the so-called 'Ulster custom', as well as different understandings of the nature and responsibility of landownership. Tenants conceived that responsibility involved certain claims on the land, ranging from the right to security of tenure and a fair rent, through to a perception of themselves as the 'rightful' owners of the soil but dispossessed by a usurping, English landlord class [58; 60]. Supporters of this more extreme view drew inspiration from the agrarian nationalist James Fintan Lalor, who popularised the notion of a peasant proprietorship. Whether these demands were valid or not, tenant farmers pressed their claims through local Tenant Protection societies, which by 1850 had federated into the Tenant League [58]. The Tenant League attracted support from all regions and denominations in Ireland, including farmers in Ulster, and even sustained a small independent Irish party at Westminster in the 1850s. Unfortunately, its non-sectarian basis, while encouraging for those who revered a non-sectarian vision of Ireland's future, aroused the wrath of both Catholic and Presbyterian interests.

Although failing to win immediate legislative redress, Tenant Right societies continued to publicise the problems of the land to a wider audience. Their struggle helped construct a representation of the land-lord class as semi-villainous, absentee, grasping, 'rack-renting' and willing to evict at will. Over the last 30 years research has shown that this was not the case [72]. Rather the Irish landlord class differed little from elsewhere, was if anything less inclined to evict or to draw the full economic value of the rent, and was composed of Catholics as well as Protestants [104]. Yet in politics reality is less important than image, and in this sense the representation became a powerful symbol for nationalists, by establishing a link between problems with the land and the evils of 'English' landlordism, and thus the evils of English rule itself. More significantly, this representation of the Irish 'question' and problems with Irish society gained widespread approval within Liberal circles. This owed a great deal to the work of the influential Liberal thinker J.S. Mill, who helped 'create the framework within which the problem was perceived' [109; 168 *p. 11*]. In other words, future Liberal governments would analyse, judge and ultimately legislate for Ireland according to images of Ireland's affairs constructed from a nationalist perspective. This was especially true of Gladstone, whose Irish reforms during his first ministry (1868–74) clearly operated under such a reading of the Irish situation

The mythical quietness of mid-nineteenth-century Ireland was also shattered by the formation in 1858 of the Irish Republican Brotherhood (IRB) or Fenian movement by James Stephens, which challenged British rule of Ireland [66; 93]. The movement was a coalition of groups that included physical-force republicans, ever watchful for the right moment to strike against the British Empire; extreme Young Irelanders, such as John O'Mahoney who in 1848 had attempted a rising in Tipperary; various local nationalist clubs such as the Emmet Monument Association and the Confederates; in addition to a host of secret agrarian societies and expatriate groups in America. Their goal was a republic won through violent means [*Doc. 3*], yet before 1865 the movement barely moved beyond fiery language and 'tap-room' insurrections. Limited in size, support, finances, central direction and encountering hostility from the Catholic Church, Fenianism is better represented as a recreational organisation, an outlet for frustrated youths, that performed a valuable role in the 'associational' culture of many local communities [65]. Indeed it is arguable that its most successful act was the funeral for the Young Irelander Terence Bellew MacManus in Dublin in 1861, stage-managed to rouse national consciousness through pathos, but also suggesting that a dead republican was of more benefit in rousing Irish opinion than a live one.

This became ever more apparent after 1865, when the IRB finally decided to make its bold strike for Irish freedom. With funds and men from America, Stephens and O'Mahoney sent Captain Kelly, a US Civil War veteran, to Ireland to prepare for a rising. However, before he could strike British agents broke up the plot, raiding IRB offices, detaining without trial many hundreds of suspects and purging IRB sympathisers from amongst Irish troops in the British army. Despite this setback, Stephens kept up pressure for a rising. In America this took the form, in May 1866, of an attack across the border into British Canada. More serious, but no less of a fiasco, in February 1867 several hundred Fenians marched on Chester Castle, only to be stopped by the local militia. A month later they attempted risings throughout Ireland, the most successful incident being the capture of a police station near Cork. Finally, in September 1867 Fenians ambushed a prison van in Manchester and rescued several of their comrades. In short, Fenian activities were small-fry. They were all acts of street theatre rather than serious revolutionary ventures, fostering myth and legend rather than representing a genuine threat to British rule. That myth was strengthened when three of the Fenians arrested after Manchester were executed. Their 'martyrdom' encouraged a wave of sympathy across Ireland, not least from the once hostile Catholic Church, which was careful to follow shifts of opinion on the ground in Ireland. In death Fenianism became powerful and able to 'turn defeat and failure into a sort of victory' [93 *p.* 74]. This most important lesson, the British authorities sturdily refused to learn.

And yet, however irksome, few of these pressures were dangerous to the Union in the way O'Connell's campaigns for emancipation and repeal had been. Britain's position in Ireland was reasonably secure, helped by the improvement in agricultural conditions, continued emigration to America over the 1850s and 1860s, and the entrenched parochialisation of Irish politics. For the vast majority of Irish people issues of tenancy, rent, food prices, grazing rights, local influence and the tithe were the important questions of politics. In addition, behind Dublin Castle stood a full array of coercive implements, from the Royal Irish Constabulary and the British Army, to a beefed up selection of legal restraints. More often Britain could rely on cooperation and collaboration. The Catholic Church was a force for stability and order, which on the whole sought reform of Catholic grievances within the Union. The growing numbers of Catholic middle classes were reasonably content, thanks to a series of government reforms since the 1840s. And even those individuals or groups that held nationalist sympathies, apart from the most extreme Fenian-type, probably imagined Ireland within some type of continued British connection. Protestant landowners and Presbyterian tenant farmers, though unhappy at the recognition given to Catholics, clung hard to the Union, aware of its importance to the preservation of their political, religious and economic power.

On the other hand, a more 'enlightened' observer might have detected signs of future trouble. Land issues, particularly between landlords and tenants, remained a 'running sore', always capable of provoking serious disturbances, as during the depression of 1859–64, and whose problems were increasingly coming to overlap with a nationalist analysis of Ireland's difficulties [58; 117]. Secondly, Irish groups abroad were becoming more vocal by the 1860s in their condemnation of British rule, and able to back their words with growing amounts of money and military experience following the US Civil War [56; 82] (nationalist sentiment had traditionally been more vigorous from the safety of another continent). In addition, nationalist theories of state organisation grew in popularity and sophistication across Europe after the upheavals of 1848–49 [299]. The unification of Italy and Germany, the Augsleich in Austria-Hungary and nationalist rumblings in the Balkans by the 1870s spread the appeal and relevance of nationalist sentiment.

PART TWO: ANALYSIS

3 GLADSTONE, PARNELL AND HOME RULE, 1869–90

By the mid-1860s, with continuing demands for reform coming from the National Association and Tenant Right League, in addition to the upsurge of Fenian violence, circumstances suggested the Act of Union between Britain and Ireland had not brought the latter the stability and prosperity promised by British politicians. Gladstone, leader of the Liberal party, sought to rectify this with a programme of reforms in education, land and Church affairs, but with only limited success. In fact the major consequence was to give rise to a nationalist movement that under Charles Stuart Parnell captured mass support from across Ireland and forced the question of Irish self-rule to the centre of British politics. Again it was Gladstone who responded to Parnell's demand by introducing a Home Rule Bill in 1886. The measure failed to reach the statute book but had an enormous impact on Anglo-Irish relations.

GLADSTONE, BUTT AND THE HOME RULE LEAGUE, 1869–74

In 1868 the new Liberal Prime Minister, William Gladstone, entered office with a 'mission to pacify Ireland' [274]. Up to this point Ireland had had a limited impact on his career, the only connection being his resignation from Peel's ministry in 1845 over the Maynooth grant, though he subsequently voted for it in the Commons. Indeed, he made his name at the Treasury, where institutional hostility towards Ireland still lingered, harking back to Trevelyan, and where free trade orthodoxies reigned. This equipped him with a blinkered and far from sensitive understanding of Irish affairs. On the other hand, Ireland was an ideal subject for his restless reformist zeal, riddled, as he believed it was, by racial differences, rural impoverishment, acrimonious social relations and religious conflict. He followed Peel's attempt to reconcile Ireland's divisions by impartial government and the removal of existing grievances, to encourage social harmony and loyalty to the

Union. He also, like Peel, looked to the existing Protestant landed elite for enlightened leadership of Irish society, but shorn of their special privileges or the advantages of birth which simply raised class barriers. As with mainland Britain, his reforms were intent on fostering a new, lean, fit, conscientious, open and meritocratic ruling class [274]. As early as 1865, he publicly expressed sympathy for disestablishing the Irish Church, followed a year later by support for an unsuccessful attempt at land reform. The Fenian terrorism of 1867 gave Gladstone an extra nudge to 'look beyond the violence at what had created the violence and to wonder if the time had not come to woo Ireland from the paths of desperation by a sustained attempt at constructive reform' [27 *p. 137*]. Come the election of 1868, he had decided his attempt to woo the Irish would consist of reform to the Irish Church, land tenure and education, the three branches of what he termed the poisonous Upas tree, areas that Peel had similarly tried and failed to tackle.

Gladstone quickly found Ireland a thornier plant than he expected, resistant to the kind of moral force and boldness of action with which he humbled other difficulties. The least controversial part of his programme, Irish Church disestablishment, was pushed through in 1869 without much political dispute, except from a group of Irish Tories angered at the dismantling of their Church. Unfortunately, the goodwill this won Gladstone in Ireland, and particularly from the Catholic Church, was squandered by failing to grant amnesty to Fenian prisoners, the demand for which had grown steadily throughout 1868–69. Irish disapproval on this issue was registered in November 1869 when the Fenian prisoner O'Donovan Rossa was elected as MP for Tipperary. From this an Amnesty Association was formed to secure the release of the remaining Fenian prisoners, and in May 1870 this developed into a Home Government Association, led by Issac Butt and dedicated to winning a mild form of self-rule for Ireland [103]. If Gladstone's Irish policy had been to 'draw a line between the Fenians and the people of Ireland, and to make the people of Ireland indisposed to cross it' [274 *p. 192*], then events of 1869–70 suggested he was largely ineffectual.

More contentious was his Land Act of 1870, which extended to the rest of Ireland the so-called Ulster custom, a tenant's 'right' to sell their interest in the holding [58]. For Bull this represented a landmark piece of legislation in recognising a 'distinctively Irish perspective' on property rights [60 *p. 54*], but it brought Gladstone few political benefits and 'was, at best irrelevant, at worst counter-productive' [108 *p. 36*]. The Act generated serious political opposition within the

Cabinet, from Whigs worried by the interference of the state into property relations and by the example it set for future legislation. It was of little benefit to tenants since landlords simply raised their rents to compensate their extra expense, while it ignored the tenants' more substantial demands for free sale, fair rent and fixity of tenure: the three Fs. In addition, though reducing the bitter class relations between tenants and landlords, the Act did not eliminate them and within a decade their simmering hostility boiled over into a full-blown land war. Gladstone's final Irish reform of the university system in 1873 upset just about everyone. In particular, the Catholic Church was dismayed by the failure to endow its denominational colleges and in protest shifted its support and influence behind the Home Government Association. The result was a government defeat on 11 March 1873, forcing Gladstone's resignation. His mission to pacify Ireland ended in failure. It brought to Ireland not social peace and political calm, but yet more furore over the land, the alienation of the Catholic Church and the emergence of a Home Government Association aimed at restructuring the Union.

Initially the Home Government Association had been led by landed Protestants, who were incensed at the destruction of their Church and interference with their rights as landlords [114]. They drew upon the Patriot nationalism of the 1780s and 1840s, and similarly calculated that a semi-independent Irish Parliament would be a safer guarantee for their interests than a British government vulnerable to shifts in party politics and so easily scared into action by Fenian violence. This strain of 'conservative nationalism' was not intent on abandoning the Union, but merely devolving power within the UK, and for Issac Butt this meant a form of federalism. However, once established, the Home Government Association quickly began to attract a wide collection of individuals and groups with nationalist sympathies [103 *p. 85*]. They included ex-O'Connellite repealers, Young Irelanders such as A.M. Sullivan and P.J. Smyth, those Fenians who had escaped prison, some Catholic middle-class elements such as publicans and clerks, and tenant farmers annoyed at the limited nature of the Land Act. This provided the Association with sufficient strength to capture a string of seats during 1872, winning County Meath in January, Galway in February, Westmeath in June and Limerick in September, where Butt himself was returned.

These successes, and its growing Catholic presence, recommended the Home Government party to the Church and the Catholic National Association as a more effective vehicle for advancing their interests. In deserting Gladstone and Liberalism for the cause of

Home Rule, a process was begun by which 'Home Rule ... (became) ... synonymous with the assertion of popular Catholic sentiment' [114 *p. 5*]. In recognition of this shift and aware of the value of clerical sympathy for winning local support, Home Government candidates now pledged themselves to denominational education. More alarming for Gladstone, many sitting Irish Liberal MPs, worried by the advance of the Home Government party and the stance taken up by the Catholic Church, drifted across to Butt. Even the IRB Supreme Council, debilitated since the disasters of 1867, placed its faith in violent insurrection on hold, to give local help to the Home Government Association [66; 93]. Expansion changed the complexion of the Association from a rather elite and conservative group of Protestant landlords into a larger, predominantly Catholic movement, forcing it to reconstitute itself as the Home Rule League. The effectiveness of the new organisation was registered at the 1874 election, when it won 60 seats across the south and west of Ireland, and reduced the Liberals to just 10. Six years of well-intentioned Gladstonian meddling had resulted in the loss of support by the Catholic Church, the collapse of Liberal power in Ireland and the rise of a strong nationalist movement the like of which had not been seen since O'Connell's repeal campaign.

Yet we must not overestimate the strength of the Home Rule League at this stage or view it as the embodiment of Irish separatism or even as much of a threat to the Union. The League was not a mass movement nor did it sweep all-Ireland under its umbrella, remaining largely a parliamentary affair, which is unsurprising given that the size of the Irish electorate was just 4.4 per cent of the population. The League was unable to offer a voice to the 'village pump' politics that still dominated the localities, with all its squabbles over land, rent-levels, prices, wages, tenure and grazing. It was also a deeply divided movement. Over half its MPs were turn-coat Irish Liberals, who retained a reverence for Gladstonian issues, while others expressed a sympathy for Irish Toryism. Some pursued their own special concerns looking for reforms on land or Church interests. Butt found it impossible to lead or coordinate such an unwieldy group and this was reflected in the Commons where League members 'spoke and voted as they pleased with an eye to their constituents rather than to any common party line' [103 *p. 215*]. Such fissures were evident when twelve Home Rulers failed to vote for Butt's amendment to the Queen's speech in 1874. More fundamentally, the movement divided over what Home Rule actually meant, a question that had earlier plagued O'Connell. Protestant Tories visualised a return to a Grattan-style Parliament of limited self-government but still firmly within the Union. Irish Liberals conceived of a larger slice of self-rule for Ireland or even a federal structure for the UK. IRB sympathisers imagined Home Rule as a mere stepping stone towards full independence and the creation of an Irish republic. Conflicting definitions of Home Rule kindled quarrels over tactics. Butt remained wedded to normal parliamentary methods, extracting reforms from British governments and advertising the need for an Irish legislature if none were forthcoming. Others, as with the small group of MPs grouped around Joe Biggar and John O'Conner Power who had IRB connections, adopted more aggressive and obstructive methods within the Commons. For them the parliamentary party should use all means at its disposal, including the disruption of business at Westminster, in order to thrust the cause of Ireland before British politicians and public alike. Such methods achieved a great deal of notoriety at Parliament and in the press, and helped bring to prominence Charles Stewart Parnell.

THE RISE OF PARNELL, 1875–80

Parnell came from a Protestant landed background, the grandson of a famous Irish Chancellor of the Exchequer who in 1799 had defended Grattan's Parliament and opposed the Act of Union. Elected MP for Meath in 1875, Parnell's energy, his family name, his aristocratic demeanour and the vigour of his attacks quickly won him recognition in Britain and Ireland [252; 273]. He gave leadership to the small band of obstructionist MPs in the Commons, imposing discipline and inspiring his troops through courageous parliamentary performances. In August 1877, with IRB support [134] and the assistance of John Devoy, leader of the American expatriate Clan na Gael, Parnell replaced the mild Butt as President of the Home Rule Confederation. What transformed his own position was the fusion of the campaign in Parliament to a wave of agrarian protest that swept across western and southern parts of Ireland after 1879, the so-called land war.

The land war was the consequence of a depression in Irish agriculture late in 1878 [58; 60; 62]. Depression cut deep into farming incomes amongst tenants in the west and amongst the larger farmers and graziers of the south, used to a fairly good standard of living during the prosperity of the 1850s and 1860s. As a consequence of falling incomes, rural unemployment rose as farmers were forced to hire fewer labourers, and urban commercial interests were hit given their reliance upon the trade and purchasing power of farmers. The poor conditions sparked a wave of unrest within the rural community which from April 1879, after a demonstration over rent arrears at Irishtown in County Mayo, was organised behind a Land League. By July the League was coordinating agitation throughout Mayo and then in October was extended into the National Land League, covering most counties of the south and west. It was led by Michael Davitt [92], an advocate of land nationalisation as a solution to Ireland's problems and whose social radicalism (what we might call left-wing nationalism) was part of a tradition within Irish nationalism going back to Young Ireland and forward to the radical nationalism of James Connolly in the 1900s. The League challenged the very basis of landlordism by resisting the payment of rent, which it enforced using techniques of communal ostracism such as the boycotting of estates, demonstrations and large open-air meetings, as well as more violent methods: threats, burning, wounding and even murder. But the League also attracted the interest of Fenians, who were well represented amongst the leadership, notably in Michael Davitt and John Devoy, and who provided vital organisational help at the local level. For Fenians the land war was a mass mobilisation of Irish men and women to be exploited to win Irish independence. Their thinking was that a British Parliament would never grant land reforms, and tenant farmers would be forced to recognise that only from a separate Irish Parliament would they see a change in Irish landholding. Agrarian pressure to win political change.

Parnell moved slowly to embrace the concerns of the Land League. The Home Rule party, though sympathetic to tenants, was not primarily concerned with land reform and as a constitutional party was worried by the political implications of associating with violence. Parnell was also deeply suspicious of Davitt's ideas on land redistribution and lacked the virulent anti-landlord sentiment of the Land League: he was after all a landlord. However, after negotiations with Davitt and Devoy during September 1879, Parnell sank his reservations and aligned himself and the party behind the League, being elected President of the National Land League in October. He now held the presidency of the Home Rule Confederation and the Land League, linking his high political campaign at Westminster with low agrarian unrest throughout Ireland in what became known as the New Departure. In a powerful speech the following autumn at Ennis he publicly embraced the League's objectives, speaking of English tyranny and targeting the landlords with a campaign of boycotting [*Doc. 4*]. These were powerful appeals which alongside his contact with known Fenians and speeches in defence of Fenian violence shocked many, particularly in the Catholic Church, and suggested that Parnell was a dangerous extremist. But several important qualifications must be added. Parnell's own views on the land problem were far from orthodox, despite the colour and tone of his rhetoric. For him, resolving tenant grievances was to remove the poison from social relations on the land and to encourage class harmony [252]. Once this was achieved the landed classes would then play their historic role at the vanguard of the Home Rule movement as leaders of Irish society. Although many thought he was trumpeting revolution, Parnell was a social conservative, motivated by a desire to preserve: land reform was 'to open up a new and better future for the Irish landlords' [252 *p. 138*], strengthening their position within Irish society. This positioned Parnell within the strain of Patriot nationalism of the 1780s and 1790s and much closer to the ideals of Grattan and Butt. Aware of these differences, Davitt and the radical elements of the League remained suspicious of Parnell. For them he was a useful 'front-man' for the organisation, bestowing respectability and a personality for people to associate with, but one whom they would be able, so they believed, to manipulate.

Whatever the differences between Parnell and Davitt, the land campaign proved of immense advantage for Parnell. Under the Home Rule banner was now mobilised the mass of Ireland's tenant farmers, agricultural labourers, and depressed urban trading interests, blending their demand for recovery of their rights over the land into the recovery of 'their' historic homeland. It brought Parnell to national prominence and strengthened his position in the party. At the 1880 election 63 Home Rulers were returned, much more unified than before and of the activist type who looked to Parnell's style of parliamentary engagement, enabling him to seize the leadership of the party from the moderates under William Shaw. Parnell bridged the party at Westminster with the struggle on the ground in Ireland, becoming the living embodiment of the nationalist struggle: a charismatic figure able to generate popular support and loyalty across Ireland. This was important since the mass movement he now led remained deeply skewed by parochial concerns, personal rivalries and class-based differences. The nationalist movement was never as unified as local agitators, contemporary ballad-makers or subsequent historians have suggested.

GLADSTONE'S SECOND MINISTRY, 1880–85

Parnell's strengthened parliamentary position and the wider land agitation he had at his command ensured Irish issues would again be brought to the attention of a British government. The fact that it was a Liberal government under Gladstone, having won the 1880 election, gave Parnell confidence that he could extract quite substantial reforms. Gladstone once again sought to mollify tensions within Irish society [150]. He was dismayed by the land war and upset by reports of evictions and hardship from overly bleak accounts by police and resident magistrates which suggested a failure of landlords to perform their social and moral obligations; to Forster he wrote of their 'unmanliness' [275 *p. 189*]. As a consequence he adopted O'Conner Powers's Compensation for Disturbance Bill which aimed to slow up the rate of eviction, only to see it defeated in the House of Lords. More successfully he established a commission on land under Lord Bessborough to look into the working of the 1870 Act. It recommended the introduction of the three Fs, which were subsequently incorporated by Gladstone into a second Land Act in 1881. The Act set up land courts to fix rents and was designed to tempt tenants away from agitation by satisfying what he regarded as their legitimate grievances. As with the 1870 Land Act, it represented an attempt to find that 'point on the scale of Irish demands (where) "a definitive settlement" of the land question could be made' [275 *pp. 192–3*]. The three Fs were, he hoped, that point of definitive settlement, although the danger of this type of analysis was that it raised expectations about what could be achieved, so shifting the point of settlement towards more radical measures. The Act brought Gladstone little political advantage. He himself had grave doubts about such extensive interference with property ownership and could only give 'hesitant, obscure and temporary' support [147 *p. 105*], finally being pushed into granting it by the radical Joseph Chamberlain. The fact that Gladstone gave way shows, as with Peel and later with Arthur Balfour, that British politicians were willing to implement legislation for Ireland that they would not dream of imposing on the mainland. The Land League resisted its implementation in Ireland, although this reflected their concern that the Act was popular amongst tenants, thus undercutting their power base. Most seriously, it alienated the Whig section of Cabinet and led to the resignation of Lords Lansdowne and Argyle. For Roy Jenkins the split marked the point of origin for the much bigger split later over Home Rule – the 'perforation along which it was easy for the Home Rule issue to tear in 1886' [269 *p. 476*].

Given Whig hostility and the continuing unrest in Ireland by the League, Gladstone accompanied land reform with measures to strengthen the coercive powers of Dublin Castle – an echo here of

Peel's earlier policy. The forthright Sir Thomas Steele assumed command of military forces in October 1880. A Peace Preservation Act was introduced in March 1881 allowing for detention without trial, and in the autumn the League was proscribed an unlawful association. More dramatically, Parnell was arrested in October 1881 in a fit of Gladstonian pique that his Land Act was not being given a fair trial. Outlawing the League and arresting Parnell were extremely ill-timed. The League's campaign was already breaking up as a consequence of a number of factors: the government's Land Act and coercive legislation, a slight improvement in agricultural conditions that took the wind from the agrarian unrest, continued leadership squabbles, hostility from the Catholic Church at what it feared was an unfolding social revolution, and the organised resistance from Property Defence Associations. The League's weaknesses had been exposed by the dismal response to its call for a rent-strike, late in 1881. In fact, the campaign against landlordism had amounted to little more than a few 'spasmodic skirmishes' [104 *p. 30*], which varied from region to region, and was largely ineffective given only 25 per cent of rents due were not paid. With the League collapsing, Parnell struggled to preserve his standing at the head of the movement. Prison, from October to May 1882, rescued him from this uncomfortable position, for nothing revived a faltering nationalist reputation like an English jail. As he told his mistress Kitty O'Shea, 'politically it is a fortunate thing for me that I have been arrested, as the movement is breaking fast and all will be quiet in a few months, when I shall be released' [252 *p. 55*].

For Gladstone, coercion and the imprisonment of Parnell undermined whatever sympathy he had won in Ireland by his reforms. To salvage the situation and win fair treatment for his Land Act, he opened discussions with Parnell in the spring of 1882 to help bring calm to Ireland. Through the intermediaries of Chamberlain and Captain O'Shea, Gladstone negotiated an agreement in May, the so-called Kilmainham treaty, whereby Parnell was released and help was given to tenants in arrears in return for a fair trial for the Land Act and an end to the rural agitation. The agreement angered Whigs and prompted Forster's resignation as Chief Secretary, but for Gladstone it encouraged closer cooperation with Parnell that developed over the next few years into a close political alliance, a 'Union of hearts'. The assassination of the new Chief Secretary, Lord Frederick Cavendish, and his Under-Secretary Burke in Phoenix Park, Dublin, on 6 May 1882, delivered relations a severe shock. Parnell denounced the crime, although attempts were made to associate him with it.

The murders reinforced the conservative drift in Parnell's actions and thinking since the autumn of 1881. With the land agitation in decline he needed fresh impetus to sustain the momentum of the nationalist movement. To this end he formed from the detritus of the Land League a new Irish National League in October 1882, hoping to avert the retreat of Irish politics back into parochialism by uniting the people around the national idea [128]. The organisation fell more firmly under Parnell's control and was committed to constitutional progress, to the point of his criticising Fenian outrages in 1883–84. It also benefited from the steady influx of money from Clan na Gael, sustaining local organisation, propaganda and the salaries of MPs. Formation of a new National League also enabled Parnell to establish a concordat with the Catholic Church. Parnell's relations with the Church had been distant, given his Protestantism and close association with Fenians and the land agitation. As he cast these aside and took on a more respectable role and organisation, from early 1882, he moved closer to the Catholic Church [257 *pp. 9–37*]. This was the vital 'recruiting-sergeant' throughout Ireland, helping to re-create a 'clerical-nationalist alliance' as existed under O'Connell and slowly 'Catholicising' nationalism after its flirtation with agrarian unrest and Fenian extremism [54 *p. 22*]. Parnell, despite his non-sectarian vision for Ireland, went far to placate the Church. His backing for the atheist Charles Bradlaugh turned to fierce condemnation after 1883, while his previous support for non-denominational education reappeared in a vigorously denominational garb. In October 1884 he was rewarded for such commitment by a public recognition from the Church that his Nationalist party was the 'agency for promoting [its] political cause' [257 *p. 22*]. The fire-eating Parnell of 1879–80 had shed his skin to reveal a constitutionally minded, Catholic-nationalist by 1884. Indeed, from this point his career would bear diminishing resemblance to his early exploits. He lived the life of an absentee landowner, residing with his mistress in London or along the south coast of England, enjoying the political game at Westminster and returning to Ireland for the grouse rather than the people; one historian has suggested that from 1885 he even 'ceased lead[ing] the party in the country' [257 *p. 25*].

This pushed things too far. Parnell by 1884 was clearly the dominant force in Irish politics, the head of a powerful National League, with the backing of the Catholic Church and a tightly disciplined party at Westminster. It enabled him to play a more effective and lucrative role in Parliament, engaging both the Liberal and Tory parties in a Dutch auction for his support. In the autumn of 1884 he negotiated with Chamberlain for some type of central board for Ireland [125; 129]. The scheme foundered on Cabinet division and Parnell's misgivings that it did not go far enough, drawing from him the famous if rather meaningless declaration that 'no man has the right to fix the boundary to the march of a nation'. Hoping for more from the Tories, and particularly when the Liberal government tried in early 1885 to renew the Crimes Act, Parnell helped unseat Gladstone's second ministry in June 1885. It brought to power Lord Salisbury at the head of a Tory ministry, and opened up one of the most interesting and complex periods in Anglo-Irish relations.

THE STRUGGLE FOR HOME RULE, 1885–86

Parnell's ability to work with Tories was based upon extracting concessions, and at a deeper level, a shared concern for a conservative solution to the land question that would maintain social relations and cure rural violence. Lord Salisbury reciprocated by dropping Gladstone's Crimes Act, and introducing a Housing Act to help labourers and an Educational Endowments Act to secure the endowment of Catholic educational concerns [145]. More surprisingly, his ministry brought in a Land Act (the Ashbourne Act) that provided state funds for tenants to buy out landlords, at cheap rates of interest. This can be interpreted as a first step towards an Irish peasant proprietorship, a move advocated by the radical Young Irelander James Fintan Lalor, and was more far-reaching than anything introduced by Gladstone. Gladstone had looked to improve the rights of tenants, thus creating a sort of dual ownership of the land to heal tenant–landlord antagonism. Tories pursued the more radical solution of buying out the Irish landlords, at attractive rates, so preserving the single ownership of the land (albeit the Irish tenants now owning it) that would (and this was essential for Tories) protect the inviolability of property rights. It was a long-term strategy to secure Britain's position in Ireland by converting the tenant farmers, through the responsibilities of property ownership, into a non-radical group that would be content within the Union. Some Tories, notably Randolph Churchill and Lords Ashbourne and Carnarvon, wanted to accompany this with a devolution of power along federal lines or even a mild form of Home Rule, but dropped the idea after encountering party resistance [113; 143]. Parnell remained optimistic that Salisbury's ministry might be manoeuvred towards Home Rule; he even recommended that Irish voters in British constituencies vote Tory at the general election of November 1885. Yet he never forgot his role as a broker for Irish interests and simultaneously angled for Gladstone's support by sending him a draft Home Rule Bill during the election contest.

The political situation was transformed by the 1885 election, to the advantage of Parnell. It was the first on the new electoral register, introduced by the Reform Acts of 1884/85, which increased the franchise in Ireland by 200 per cent and brought the newly politicised tenant farmers into the electorate [9; 54 *ch 1*]. The Reform Acts had not, however, introduced a thorough-going redistribution of seats according to population, so providing Ireland with approximately 20–30 extra seats for which her post-famine population size did not qualify her. The result of these developments was that Liberals returned 333 MPs, though for the first time none from Ireland, while Tories returned 250 MPs and in Ireland were left high and dry on just sixteen seats from Ulster plus two for Dublin University. Home Rulers, on the other hand, were triumphant across much of Ireland, gaining 85 seats, and one in Liverpool, that furnished Parnell with a truly mass movement in Ireland and the balance of power at Westminster. He held back from immediate action and kept his own counsel as to what he would accept in return for his party's support. In this way he hoped to win a larger degree of self-rule for Ireland by playing both parties off against each other.

The election had a powerful effect on Gladstone, crystallising his vague speculations on Irish affairs into an awareness that some form of self-government for Ireland was unavoidable [125 *p. 242*]. This change in attitude owed something to his long-standing support for struggling nations and to a belief in the ideal of a Liberal Commonwealth, where imperial powers acted as a civilising force, duty bound to 'prepare colonies for independence and self government' [106, *p. 62*]. More immediately, Gladstone interpreted the 1885 result as representing the settled and mature opinion of the Irish people, and Parliament was thus morally bound to satisfy that opinion. The danger was, as he realised, that if left unsatisfied Nationalist representatives might in any case secede from Westminster. This would present government with the awful choice of coercing Ireland back under the Union or acquiescing in the change, either option being liable to dent the standing of the British Parliament. A far safer course, as Gladstone realised, was for bold action now to avert a more serious colonial entanglement. Such views were in line with his earlier actions that had sought the minimum point at which Irish grievances could be settled while preserving the existing social order and Act of Union. By 1885 that point was now Home Rule and Gladstone responded by drawing the issue into 'practical politics'. Tactical considerations also played a part in Gladstone's thinking, not least the numerical importance of Parnell's 86 MPs to any Gladstone ministry in the future. More cynically still, one famous account paints Gladstone raising a new Liberal crusade around Home Rule for Ireland as a 'device' to sideline Chamberlain and his radical Liberalism that by late 1885 was challenging Gladstone's supremacy in the party [113]. Home Rule enabled him to steer the party back to more traditional Liberal pursuits and, simultaneously, reinforce his own indispensability as leader. Few historians would now go this far, preferring to see Gladstone's commitment as a balance between low political cunning and high-minded morality. Gladstone was a leader of principle who also had to operate in an environment where such 'political' considerations were the essential tools of power.

Unfortunately, however well-reasoned his reading of the situation, Gladstone realised his proposal would alienate important Whig sections of the Liberal party grouped around Lord Hartington [*Doc. 5*]. These sections feared that Home Rule was a stepping stone to full independence, likely to destabilise the United Kingdom, endanger her coastal defences, and threaten the religious liberties and property of Irish Protestants by imposing what in effect would be a Catholic assembly over them. Gladstone needed time to break this resistance down, operating what he told the Foreign Secretary Granville would be 'a healthful, slow fermentation of many minds' [269 *p. 522*], while remaining hopeful that the Tories might bring forward legislation for Irish self-government as a means to bolster their minority in the Commons. Given the delicacy of circumstances, the Hawarden Kite of 17 December 1885, where Gladstone's son Herbert briefed the press on his father's conversion to Home Rule, was distinctly unhelpful. It allowed Whig opposition to consolidate against the move while simultaneously driving a wedge between Parnell and the Tories. Tory strategy now faced the choice of out-bidding Gladstone by granting Home Rule, a turn liable to split the party, or of reconstituting their policy in a more rigidly pro-Union direction and hoping to win public support by playing on deep-rooted, anti-Irish and anti-Catholic sentiment [133; 204]. When Carnarvon resigned from the Cabinet on 16 January 1886 and W.H. Smith, the new Irish Chief Secretary, advocated a Coercion Bill a week later, the Tory government signalled its choice. Aware that Home Rule would not be extracted from Salisbury, Parnell now crossed sides and joined with the Liberals to defeat his government. Gladstone returned to power for a third time, in January 1886, pledged to a still undefined measure of self-rule for Ireland. A gaggle of Whigs, as well as the radical Bright, refused office under him and instead adopted an independent position in the House of Commons. To much surprise, Chamberlain agreed to serve even though he was hostile to Home Rule. He hoped to use what influence he had to modify the bill towards federalism, but failed to make any headway and resigned from the Cabinet in March.

The Home Rule Bill was introduced by Gladstone on 8 April 1886 [*Doc. 6*]. It proposed a unicameral legislature with an upper house composed of 103 members, elected on a property franchise and with the power to veto for three years, and a lower house of 206 members elected on a popular franchise. The legislature would have charge of all legislation except that relating to the Crown, peace and war, military forces, honours, foreign relations, trade, navigation, customs and excise, coinage and copyright, while its fiscal powers were narrowly circumscribed. The legislature was responsible to an executive, nominally the Lord Lieutenant, who would act on the advice of an Irish Cabinet sitting in the lower chamber. The scheme followed colonial precedents in that the Irish Parliament was subservient to the Imperial Parliament, with Irish representatives unable to sit at Westminster (though they would in the Home Rule Bills of 1893 and 1912), and executive authority vested in the Crown.

The bill faced sizeable parliamentary opposition, from the entire Tory party, a Whig group under Hartington and a small radical break-away led by Chamberlain [131]. On 7 June 1886 these political groupings combined to defeat Home Rule by 343 votes to 313. Of this, 93 Liberals had voted against their leader. Gladstone, exasperated and indignant, was granted an election for July, hopeful that he could swing the country behind him. Unfortunately Gladstonian Liberals slumped to just 191 seats. With 86 Parnellites also returned, this gave the supporters of Home Rule a parliamentary presence of about 270. Against this stood 314 opponents or Unionists, comprising Tories and 72 'seceding' Liberals, Liberal Unionists. Gladstone's hope of rousing the British people behind Home Rule was dealt a mortal blow: Gladstone himself represented it as 'a smash' [269 *p. 530*]. It certainly had far-reaching consequences. For British politics a major re-configuration took place. The Liberal party was irretrievably split. Liberal Unionists moved into alliance with Tories and after 1895 into government with them: a combination that would dominate government for the next 20 years. For Ireland the change was less clear-cut. Unionist administration in Ireland, though determined to uphold law and order, followed a fairly constructive course that echoed Peel's 1841–46 ministry and to some extent resembled the direction, if not the style, of Gladstone. For Parnell 1886 represents the high point of his career. He had converted one of the two great parties of state to

Home Rule for Ireland. He had brought Ireland 'within sight of the promised land', and if the struggle for Catholic emancipation was any guidance, then Home Rule would be won within a generation. He had constructed a mass movement that swept into its ranks the majority of Catholic Irish voters throughout Ireland, except the small Protestant enclaves in north-east Ulster and Dublin University. It was a movement that, uniquely in Ireland's history, sustained a broad social constituency that included tenant farmers, graziers, agricultural labourers, alongside numbers of urban workers and middle-class professionals.

A NEW LANDSCAPE, 1886–90

And yet there is a sense that 1886 marked the beginning of decline for Parnellite nationalism. Despite his obvious successes, Parnell was in a difficult situation after 1886. He no longer held the balance of power at Westminster and was prohibited from the kind of 'brokering' politics that proved so rewarding between 1880 and 1885 by the Liberal–Nationalist alliance. Moreover, the failure to win Home Rule, combined with the return of agricultural depression by late 1886, encouraged radicals within the nationalist movement towards another land agitation, the so-called Plan of Campaign. Parnell was keen to preserve his contacts with the Church and Liberal party and to maintain Home Rule as the central political focus of Irish aspirations. He therefore kept aloof from the campaign, although this proved awkward given widespread nationalist sympathy for it. His position was made all the more unpleasant by attempts in *The Times* to associate him with the murder of Lord Cavendish and Burke, and by a growing anxiety at the public disclosure of his long-standing affair with Kitty O'Shea. This finally came in November 1890, when her husband filed for divorce and cited Parnell as co-respondent, an accusation he did not contest. The revelations alienated Liberal opinion, forcing Gladstone to declare an end to cooperation with the Nationalist party if Parnell remained its leader, an ultimatum that split the party into Parnellite and anti-Parnellite factions [154]. To make matters worse, the Catholic Church declared against Parnell. The nationalist leader fought to recover his power, reverting back to earlier Fenian extremism and violent rhetoric, now even tinged with traces of republicanism, in an effort to recapture public support. Much of the IRB, including John Devoy and James Stephens, lined up behind him to oppose the majority of the old Irish parliamentary party, led by a Church-backed leadership composed of Parnell's former loyal lieutenants, Tim Healy,

John Dillon and William O'Brien. It was all to no avail and Parnell died early in October 1891 while campaigning in Ireland to recover his position.

Thus Parnell's career ended in bitterness, social exclusion and failure. Home Rule was never won. Irish opinion turned against him, aided in no small measure by hostility from the Catholic Church. The National League was shattered and the Liberal–Nationalist alliance was, for the time being, destroyed. The reforms squeezed from Gladstone on land and Church matters were far less significant than Tory reforms of the 1890s, long after Parnell. He left no heir apparent and perhaps most seriously, and something he later acknowledged, he failed to appease or even take at all seriously the position of Protestants throughout Ireland and in Ulster particularly.

The development of a strong, Catholic nationalism under Parnell was mirrored in the consolidation of an oppositional movement amongst Protestants [111; 112; 118]. The Protestant counter-movement was composed of Anglo-Irish landowners and Presbyterian tenant farmers and workers from Ulster. Such dissimilar groups had little to unify them except a common suspicion of Catholicism and fear of self-rule for Ireland, on the grounds that this would place political power in the hands of the Catholic majority. Such power would endanger their religious freedoms and threaten the existing basis of property ownership in Ireland, since they believed Catholics still coveted the land stolen from them during the sixteenth and seventeenth centuries [*Doc. 7*]. In other words, Protestant fear of Irish self-rule was rooted in sentiments born of past struggles and ancient misdeeds that continued to sustain a deep communal mistrust and religious conflict. In addition, placing power into the hands of poor, unpropertied Catholics would expose Ireland's industrial and financial interests, much of which were centred in Ulster and held by Protestants, to the danger that they might well demand an improvement in their own economic well-being at the expense of Protestants. For Protestants, only by remaining in Union with Britain, as part of a larger Protestant community with intimate and strong economic connections to the British mainland, would their interests be properly secured. Thus Unionism at its core was a defensive creed, supported by those who perceived they would lose out by the introduction of Home Rule, corresponding in the main to the Protestant sections of Irish society [35].

Before 1885, the unity of the Protestant Unionist alliance should not be over-stressed; it is important to remember that the alliance remained an unstable mix of distinct interests, which was always liable to divide without the threat from Catholic nationalism. But as a result of the 1885 election, giving the Irish Nationalist party 85 seats and the balance of power at Westminster, Unionism was forced to organise itself as a political force. In Parliament Irish Tories cohered into an Irish Unionist party with support from the House of Lords and the British Conservative party. And across Ireland, through the press and local defence groups, such as the Irish Loyal Union, the Orange Order, the Irish Loyal and Patriotic Union and various Unionist clubs, Unionists drew under their banner a wide constituency of supporters [111]. This included business interests, fearful that a nationalist parliament would raise taxes, drive away investment and disrupt their exports, industrial workers in Belfast fearful about their jobs, farmers uneasy about their farms being returned to Catholic tenants, and landlords worried about their land and position within society. These fears were most pronounced amongst the Presbyterians in north-east Ulster, whose defensive mentality was given added sharpness by a long history of sectarian violence with the Catholic communities that lived amongst them [118; 124]. For Ulstermen and women, living with the 'enemy' required extra vigilance and more vigorous defensive measures, especially when a British government led by Gladstone was poised to deliver Ireland into the hands of the Catholic, Nationalist party. Moreover, this heightened sense of defensiveness was underpinned by the Protestants of Ulster having a degree of cultural, geographic and economic homogeneity that enabled them to imagine for themselves, with some persuasion, a separate regional or ethnic identity: some even regarded Ireland as a land composed of two nationalisms. Theirs was a nationalism or regional identity that, like any other, could motivate its supporters in its defence.

With the defeat of Home Rule in June 1886, the immediate threat subsided. But it left a legacy of betrayal and disloyalty that sustained Unionist organisations in Ireland, if at a lower level of readiness, ever vigilant for the next assault on their rights and freedoms. Events of 1886 also left a legacy inside Parliament, where cooperation between Tories, Irish Unionists and Liberal seceders to defeat Home Rule led to the formation of the Unionist alliance at the election of July 1886. This accord continued in the new Parliament, with Salisbury's second ministry reliant upon the support of Liberal Unionists [116; 133]. Yet it could at times be an acrimonious arrangement. Liberal Unionists were not simply Tories of a lighter hue, a few stages on in the evolutionary scale, but individuals of discrete values, with support in constituencies, not least within Ulster itself, and drawn from the mainstream of Liberalism. Few of them relished co-habitation with Salisbury, with little in common apart from defence of the Union.

And differences in style and approach quickly surfaced over Irish policy, as became apparent in the government's handling of the Plan of Campaign. The Tory Chief Secretary, Arthur Balfour, was determined to break the agitation and on taking office passed the Criminal Law and Procedure Act [156; 170]. The Act was intended to speed up the process of law. Unfortunately its enforcement in areas affected by agrarian unrest provoked riots, as at Mitchelstown on 9 September 1887 resulting in the death of two protesters. Liberal Unionists recoiled from such draconian methods, forcing Salisbury to mollify Liberal sensibilities by extending the terms of the 1881 Land Act to leaseholders and reducing levels of rent by revising downwards the rate set by the land courts. In addition, the Ashbourne land purchase scheme of 1885 was extended in 1888 and 1891, to the tune of an extra £30 million. Balfour's policy of coercion and conciliation blunted the Plan of Campaign and kept both wings of the Unionist alliance together. It was, however, an unstable relationship, prone to splits and requiring fresh threats to the Union to cement it back together. Gladstone's brief fourth ministry (1892–94) and his unsuccessful attempt to pass another Home Rule Bill was just the type of threat the Unionist alliance needed.

4 NEW DIRECTIONS, 1890–1909

The period from the death of Parnell to the introduction of a third Home Rule Bill in 1912 was once regarded as of little significance in any account of Anglo-Irish relations. James Joyce in his short story *The Dead* represents *fin de siècle* Ireland as frozen under a blanket of falling snow, while Conor Cruise O'Brien refers to it as a 'featureless valley' [153]. Without Parnell the splintered nationalist coalition lost direction and appeal, plunging into petty squabbling, with Home Rule becoming just a distant memory. More recently historians have suggested the period was one of exciting developments and fresh opportunities: a period when traditional ideas and structures, established since the 1870s, were challenged by new interests and concerns. Unfortunately, the ferment did not last. Traditionalism reasserted itself in readiness for a renewal of the 'old' fight, as Home Rule returned to the centre of British politics by 1910.

FRAGMENTATION AND THE SURVIVAL OF CONSTITUTIONAL NATIONALISM

After 1886 circumstances were far from auspicious for the Nationalist party in Parliament. The loss of their parliamentary strength, following the 1886 general election, left the Unionist coalition dominant: indeed not until 1910 would Nationalists again hold sufficient power in the Commons to force Irish issues onto a British government. The strength of Unionism offered little hope of Home Rule in the near future. For even though Gladstone returned to lead a minority government in 1892, his second attempt to pass Home Rule in 1893, which passed the House of Commons, was overwhelmingly rejected by the Unionist-dominated House of Lords. As a result of this, along with Gladstone's retirement a year later and replacement by the unsympathetic Lord Rosebery, Westminster lost its appeal as the arena in which to win Irish freedom.

These set-backs in the parliamentary sphere were compounded by the disintegration of the Irish Nationalist party, following Parnell's expulsion from the leadership in December 1890 [154]. Without his unifying authority over the nationalist movement old resentments reappeared and the party split into Parnellite and anti-Parnellite factions. The Parnellite wing shared a common legacy, centred on Parnell himself, that sustained their independent presence. The anti-Parnellites, on the other hand, lacked such an established inheritance and were forced to re-organise themselves into the Irish National Federation, under the nominal leadership of Justin McCarthy. Division between the two wings devolved into what Lyons has called 'a semi-secret, half veiled vendetta' [132 *p. 83*]. It centred upon personality and religious sensibilities, personified in the clash between Parnell and Tim Healy, 'the fiery, scurrilous, ruthless, populistic Catholic Nationalist' [33 *p. 29*]. Healy attacked Parnell with a venom born of a once close friendship, characterising him as unfit to lead the Irish nation because of his immorality, his demagoguery and his Protestantism [259]. Yet the split was also tactical; anti-Parnellites placed the continuation of their alliance with the Liberal party above the personal interests of their fallen leader. This exposed them to the famous sobriquet after Parnell's premature death in October 1891, that Ireland's lost leader had been 'sacrificed by Irishmen on the altar of English Liberalism' [132 *p. 82*]. Ironically, this accusation by the Parnellite wing carried less weight with wider Irish public opinion, at least outside Dublin, than it did amongst the squabbling party leaders. For at the general election of 1892, Parnellite candidates under the leadership of John Redmond returned just nine MPs, against an anti-Parnellite tally of 71.

Having reduced the Parnellite faction to a rump, squabbles now broke out within the National Federation. Rivalry between the two ablest leaders of the Federation, Tim Healy and John Dillon, spilled over into arguments about parliamentary candidatures, the membership of the Federation's ruling committee and the amalgamation of rival nationalist newspapers [259; 272]. At its core, differences between Healy and Dillon were over the direction for Irish nationalism in the aftermath of Parnellism. Healy looked to strengthen ties between politics and the Catholic Church, envisaging a party to champion a Catholic populism, whereas Dillon sought a centralised and disciplined party machine led by an elite group of parliamentarians, as existed under Parnell. The discord between them became so bad that at the 1895 general election Healyite candidates opposed Dillonite ones, in a bitter contest for control of the party. It ended in

Dillon replacing McCarthy as chairman of the Federation and the expulsion of Healy from the party, who went on to form his own People's Rights Association in 1897.

Nationalist politics, then, were certainly factionalised. But to extrapolate from this a period of frustrated ambitions, collapsing public faith for constitutional avenues and political paralysis is seriously to misread the situation. At Westminster Parnellites and anti-Parnellites often voted together and were able to offer strong parliamentary opposition. And on the ground in Ireland, a diversity of opinion and outlook within nationalist politics was probably a source of strength, enabling it to attract a much wider and mixed constituency of supporters than a more narrowly based, disciplined party ever could [153; 168]. However much the party looked a ramshackle motley crew, what Foster describes as a group of 'Trollopian fixers, political journalists, respectable ex-Fenians and closet imperialists' [23 *p. 265*], their political standing in Ireland remained vibrant and constant, testiment perhaps to the deep political roots Parnellite nationalism had established in Irish society during the 1880s. This was reflected in a stable electoral performance, winning 81 seats at the 1892 election and 82 at both the 1895 and 1900 elections. This was maintained after the party re-unified in January 1900, capturing 83 seats at the 1906 election, 82 in January 1910 and 84 in December 1910 [9]. Nationalists kept a tight grip on local politics, aided by continued support from the Catholic Church, and after 1898 by the introduction of the Irish Local Government Act, providing the party with enormous political influence at a village level.

Such a powerful presence suggests Ireland did not 'turn' from constitutional politics with the demise of Parnell. And in any case little serious political alternative to the Nationalist party existed in Ireland; even the handful of radical anti-British groups, such as Cumann na nGaedheal and Sinn Féin, which emerged at the turn of the century, committed themselves to change through the established political process. Only the Fenian movement retained a commitment to physical force, although this was as much a 'verbal commitment ... as an ideological one' [23 *p. 271*]. Active Fenians remained a marginal group within Irish politics, lacking the support, the finance and the determination to re-direct Irish nationalism towards militant republicanism.

Far from being a declining force by 1900, the future prospects of the Nationalist party looked pretty good. The centenary celebrations of the 1798 Rising, though accompanied by the inevitable wrangling, revived popular nationalist sentiment and helped pull the two wings of the party closer together. This was aided by the Anglo-South African war (1899–1902), another example of British imperial aggression, which united Parnellite and anti-Parnellite in common cause. Yet more significant to party fortunes was a revival of agrarian unrest. Agitation over the land had long put wind into nationalist sails. Unrest, from the mid-1890s, was fuelled by renewed depression in agriculture [60; 152]. It hit the small-holders in the west the hardest, whose impoverishment was blamed on 'land-grabbing' by rich graziers. Sporadic agitations against graziers spread quickly, demanding the break-up of the large ranches through compulsory land purchase and redistribution. By 1898 Michael Davitt and William O'Brien, MP for Cork City and a radical agrarian reformer, channelled the protest behind a United Irish League (UIL) [171]. The League orchestrated campaigns of passive resistance against graziers and landlords that grew into a mass organisation, with membership of the UIL rising from 33,000 in 1899 to 100,000 by 1901. The agitation even extended to Ulster where the maverick Liberal Unionist MP, T.W. Russell, led a separate campaign for compulsory land redistribution, but with links to O'Brien's League, that caused a great deal of alarm amongst the Protestant landed elites throughout the province [163]. By 1903 the UIL had broadened its appeal by taking on a distinctly nationalist flavour which, as before with the Land League, linked agrarian protest to political pressure for Home Rule [60; 171]. It incorporated within the movement an increasingly wide cross-section of society, enabling O'Brien to mobilise a popular mass movement, to rival anything Parnell had done in the 1870s and 1880s. Indeed the threat posed by the UIL to the power and position of the Nationalist party in Ireland was sufficient to force the Parnellite and anti-Parnellite wings to re-unify formally in 1900, under the leadership of John Redmond. The UIL now placed its organisation and support at the disposal of the reconstituted parliamentary party, securing its position as the dominant political force throughout Ireland.

IRELAND UNDER THE TORIES, 1887–1905

Tory government of Ireland has suffered at the hands of historians, from an over-concentration upon Gladstone and his high publicity attempts to solve the Irish question. Yet it is instructive to remember that the Tory governments of Salisbury (1886–92; 1895–1902) and Balfour (1902–5) were in charge of Ireland for longer than Gladstone. Nor was their legislative record inconsiderable, as the few excellent studies of their stewardship indicate [156; 159]. But they clearly approached matters differently; for where Gladstone sought political solutions to Ireland's problems, Unionists offered policies of economic regeneration in Ireland, in an effort to place British rule on a firmer and more popular basis. This broke with Salisbury's earlier recommendation for 'twenty years of firm government' for Ireland and moved Irish policy back towards Carnarvon and Churchill's progressive Conservative approach of the mid-1880s. This was a line better suited to the preservation of their alliance with Liberal Unionists at Westminster [133; 204], and was more in harmony with the calm atmosphere in Ireland during the 1890s. Of course at its core, economic regeneration was intended to 'draw the sting' from Irish nationalism; Tories believed nationalist protest was little more than the scream of the outcast and hungry, nurtured and sustained by economic backwardness. In this, British Tories acted like other European ruling elites, who were beginning to realise that the alleviation of poverty through state aid and massaging economic growth was a means to appease an advancing and increasingly restless democracy. Accordingly, from the late 1880s onwards a series of Tory Irish Chief Secretaries, first Arthur Balfour (1887–91), then his brother Gerald (1895–1900) and finally George Wyndham (1900–05), introduced a package of reforms known rather simplistically as 'Killing Home Rule with Kindness'. In reality Irish policy was more disjointed, pragmatic and responsive to events on the ground and at Westminster than such a bland label implies [159].

Whatever its origins, the catalogue of Tory reform was impressive. A Congested Districts Board (1891) was instituted to develop local infrastructure, such as railways and harbours, to promote small manufacturing concerns, and to consolidate landholdings into viable economic units. A Department of Agriculture and Technical Education was created to spread modern capitalist farming methods. These changes required rationalising local government, so in 1898 a Local Government Act established elected county councils. This was a measure Lyons describes as 'not far short of revolutionary' in that it ended the local political power of landed elites in the countryside, in favour of councils largely dominated by the Nationalists [27 *p. 212*]. Often state initiatives were performed in conjunction with voluntary and self-help groups. The formation of the Irish Agricultural Organisation Society by Horace Plunkett was one such example, helping to nurture various cooperative schemes, the most famous being the cooperative creameries [164]. But the most far-reaching Tory reforms, in the degree of social change brought to Ireland, were a series of Land Acts beginning in 1887 with the strengthening of land courts. This was followed by extensions to land purchase in 1891, 1897 and 1903. The last of these, Wyndham's Land Act, finalised the transfer of land from a Protestant Ascendancy class to a Catholic tenant farmer class, so undertaking a far more radical re-structuring of Irish life than anything Gladstone, with his high-sounding moralism, ever achieved for Ireland [152]. Wyndham's Land Act, in conjunction with the Irish Local Government Act, brought revolutionary change to Irish society. The Protestant Ascendancy was effectively wrapped up, political power now shifted decisively towards the Nationalist party and land was distributed to a growing tenant class. It marked the end of a process of readjustment of land problems begun under Peel, and continued through Gladstone and Balfour. After Wyndham, land would never again occupy the same position in Anglo-Irish politics as it had throughout the nineteenth century. The logic of this for British governments was that without such a burning grievance, the demand for Home Rule would collapse and Ireland would settle down to life under the Union. Unfortunately, for many others the logic of the situation ran in the opposite direction; with no economic or social 'interest' to defend in Ireland there was nothing now to stop the grant of Home Rule. Such a view neglected the position of the Presbyterians in north-east Ulster.

NEW DIRECTIONS, 1890–1900

The general sterility of the political struggle at Westminster and the settling of old controversies in Ireland encouraged the growth of new concerns and interests amongst the politically minded. One new focus was the growth of a Labour movement, albeit a very weak one [167]. This was no mean achievement given the limited spread of Irish manufacturing, the preponderance of semi-skilled and unskilled employment and a saturated labour market, which made unionisation very difficult. Despite these handicaps, a conference in 1894 saw the establishment of an Irish Trades Union Congress (ITUC), backed by some 119 delegates [157]. By 1900 60,000 workers were represented, although most of these also remained affiliated to British trades unions and were of a rather conservative outlook. Still there was enough interest for James Connolly, newly arrived in Dublin from Edinburgh, to establish an Irish Socialist Republican party in 1896, which married the twin themes of his career, socialism and nationalism [*Doc. 8*]. On the other hand, Belfast, with its shipbuilding, engineering and linen mills, was an advanced industrial city of 350,000, where Labour politics had already established themselves. Under the leadership of William Walker, secretary of the ITUC, organisation spread to most of the skilled and semi-skilled trades, with some movement towards general unions by the 1890s [84]. And in 1893 a branch of the Independent Labour party was formed in Belfast.

These were all modest beginnings and it would not be until the arrival of James Larkin from Liverpool in 1907 that the Irish Labour movement would finally burst into life. Larkin set about organising the dockers of Belfast into the National Union of Dock Labourers, which later spread to Dublin. Larkin's dynamism prompted a series of strikes through 1908 and laid the groundwork for the creation of the Irish Transport and General Workers' Union (ITGWU), with James Connolly emerging as leader of the Belfast branch by 1911 [278]. Both Larkin and Connolly gave Labour disputes an edge, particularly Connolly with his revolutionary socialist views and syndicalist methods, which played such an important role during the Dublin lock-out of 1913 [166; 250; 251]. Interestingly, developments in Labour politics showed, as earlier with the tenant farmer movement of T.W. Russell, that bridges across the sectarian divide in Ireland could be built. Perhaps politics in Ireland *could* advance in directions other than along Unionist or nationalist lines?

A second interest to grow over the 1890s lay with explorations into the question of *who* and *what* constituted Ireland and Irishness, or, as the Young Irelander Sir Charles Gavan Duffy once asked, 'what do we hope to make of Ireland?' [286 *p. 63*]. This movement of enquiry into Irishness took many forms, from a revival in Gaelic sports and language, to research into Irish folk-tales, right through to attempts by writers and thinkers to define the essence of Irishness. Such explorations of nationality (and ethnicity) were part of a general European movement amongst emergent nations of the late nineteenth century to quantify and differentiate their national identity, so as to provide authenticity and purpose to their national political campaign [299]. But interest in these subjects can also be linked to Parnell. His concern had always been for the purely tactical, parliamentary dilemmas of winning Home Rule, ignoring any clear definition of what self-government meant or, indeed, what it meant to be Irish. With the splintering of Parnellite nationalism from 1890, these definitional issues rose to the surface.

One institution that took a keen interest in defining Irishness was the Catholic Church. The Church had long sought to correlate Irish with Catholic, in order to maintain its dominant role as guide to Ireland's moral and political conscience [160]. Secular or Protestant varieties of Irishness were accordingly viewed with deep suspicion, notably Fenian republicanism and Parnellism. The latter had, from the late 1880s, increasingly ranked a commitment to nation above that to religion, while associating the nationalist movement with cosmopolitan values and sexual scandal. The Church looked to purge the movement of these elements by 'Catholicising' the Nationalist party and the idea of Irishness itself, in a collaboration not witnessed since the early days of Parnell or even the emancipation campaign of O'Connell [33]. This process was championed from within the party by Tim Healy and outside it by the astringent pen of D.P. Moran in his weekly journal *The Leader*, and was reflected in the country by a growing popular interest in Catholic sectarian groups such as the Catholic Association of Ireland and the Ancient Order of Hibernians [276]. For these individuals and groups the identity of the 'people-nation' [286 *pp. 58–88*] was inextricably woven into their Catholic being; as Moran wrote in 1901, 'the Irish nation is de facto a Catholic nation, just as the English Catholic recognises that England is a Protestant nation' [33 *p. 59*]. Of course, by defining Irishness as exclusively Catholic, significant 'Irish' groups on the island of Ireland were consciously denied a place within it.

While the Church looked to 'Catholicising' Irishness, other groups dedicated themselves to Gaelicising it or what MacDonagh calls 'the Irishing of Ireland' [89 *p. 72*]. They included the Gaelic League, founded after a speech by Douglas Hyde to the Irish Literary Society in 1892, in which he called for the cultural purification of Ireland from English influences, a process he termed 'de-Anglicanisation' [161]. Hyde was joined by the academic Eoin MacNeill and Father Eugene O'Growney, who together worked to bring Gaelic culture back to an Irish people who were rapidly losing it [*Doc. 9*]. On the ground the League was run by a dedicated if rather dour band of enthusiasts (like the young Patrick Pearse) who proselytised the Gaelic language through lectures, journals, pamphlets, textbooks and summer-schools and by forcing it into the Irish national curriculum. They also revived Gaelic songs and poems, hoping to re-create a once pure and unified Gaelic culture that had, they believed, thrived before English 'cultural pollution' [286 *p. 5*]. Whether consciously or not, interest in cultural revival had a significant political impact. For the League gave Irish nationalism a racial purpose; it was no longer just a movement to recover lost political rights, as it had been under Parnell, but one now intent on the revival of the Irish race itself. This fortified nationalism with a stronger claim to hold sole authority over the land and people of Ireland. And if proof were needed, remnants of this older Gaelic Ireland were thought still to exist in parts of the west of

Ireland, which came to represent a living symbol of a society all but eradicated by the British: a sort of 'cultural homeland' [287 *p. 7*]. For middle-class Gaelic revivalists like Pearse, summer vacations amongst the culturally rich landscape and labourers of the west were little short of a pilgrimage. Yet this again was not a unique development, for the injection of racial theories into nationalist ideas placed the Irish experience firmly within a wider European setting.

Along similar lines, though on a much larger scale, the Gaelic Athletic Association (GAA) was founded by Michael Cusack to revive Gaelic sports, such as hurling, while simultaneously 'boycotting' English games like cricket: a method that suggests an overlap with the techniques of the land war [91; 161; 165]. Through its extensive local network of branches, the GAA acquired a mass following that transmitted new ideas and values to a wide Irish audience. It also attracted the attention of Fenians, quick to discern its political and military potential; extending Gaelic sports would foster, they imagined, a strong manhood conscious of its own Irishness and eager for battle with the English. Yet much of the support for both the Gaelic League and the GAA owed less to a vibrant anti-Britishness than to economic and generational changes: the emergence of 'a young and ambitious intelligentsia', frustrated by the collapse of Parnellite nationalism and an 'excess of socially aspiring educated lower middle class Catholics', frustrated by the lack of employment opportunities in an Ireland where Anglo-Irish Protestants still dominated socio-economic power [162 *pp. 100–19*].

And from yet another direction, an Irish Literary Revival explored Gaelic myths and legends in books and on the stage, crafting a common Gaelic literature they hoped would bind both Irish Protestant and Irish Catholic together. Through the National Literary Society, founded in 1892, and the Abbey Theatre of 1898, the work of W.B. Yeats, Lady Gregory, George Moore and J.M. Synge sought to bring together the wide religious, social and regional diversity of Ireland behind a shared Gaelic heritage: a heritage that would be 'a meeting ground for Irishmen of diverse political persuasions, and to lessen, perhaps even destroy, political and sectarian conflict in Ireland' [14 *p. 121*]. Not the least part of this common Gaelic heritage would be a common history. Accordingly, the Literary Revival invented and exalted stories of a glorious Gaelic past, of Irish warriors vanquishing strangers in their land and of the noble peasant upholding traditional values, as a means of creating a common, unifying past; a shared history to inculcate a sense of togetherness and similarity. Furthermore, to help craft a common Gaelic identity, Yeats, in his writings, used a sense of place and landscape. He gloried in the unspoilt pastoral landscape of the west of Ireland (his 'Sligo idyll') [300 *p. 102*], and compared it to the grey, urban and industrial environment of Britain. By drawing upon perceptions of place and landscape, Yeats invested the Irish character with qualities of purity, strength and traditionalism, irrespective of religious differences, and distinguished it from an Englishness that was corrupted, immoral, unnatural [297].

Yet it was not just in nationalist Ireland that questions of identity were debated, for Unionism was also affected by tensions about what it was and what it stood for or against. Unionism had always been an unstable mix of British Conservatives, Liberal Unionists, southern Irish landowning Anglicans, alongside Presbyterian and predominantly working-class loyalists centred in Ulster [20; 181]. As divisions within the nationalist movement and the retirement of Gladstone removed the threat of Home Rule, so Unionist forces found it difficult to remain bound together. This fragmentation was hastened by the retreat of Unionism throughout the south and west of Ireland, as its economic and political power collapsed with the attack on Irish landlordism from the Local Government Act and Wyndham's Land Act [111]. These developments raised several questions: if Unionism in the south had lost its political and economic strength, what arguments could Unionists now reasonably deploy against Home Rule, and how would they resist its future introduction? More crucially, what was Unionism now defending: was it still a movement to maintain the link between Britain and *all*-Ireland or did it now reflect the altered economic and political realities and seek to preserve just those areas where Unionists were dominant, namely Ulster. The notion of a monolithic, all-Irish Unionism was largely a fiction by 1900, still useful in political rhetoric though without much basis in actuality [124; 173; 204].

But even within the strongest part of Unionism, that centred around Ulster, changes over the 1890s and early 1900s revealed it to be a precarious coalition of different identities. The growth of the Labour movement in Belfast threatened to subvert the hegemony of loyalism with a vision centred upon class and differences of wealth. In a similar fashion T.H. Sloan founded an Independent Orange Order in 1903, as a radical working-class alternative to the landlord-dominated official Orange Order [124]. But most serious and divisive was T.W. Russell's organisation of tenant farmers, with links to O'Brien's United Irish League [163]. Russell, a Liberal Unionist MP for South Tyrone, championed a populist brand of Unionism that embraced the compulsory purchase of land. During 1902–03 at a series of by-elections, he ran Independent Unionist candidates against the landlord-dominated Ulster party, winning seats in East Down, South Tyrone and North Fermanagh. Indeed it was pressure from Russell, on both Balfour's government and upon the Ulster Unionist party, that influenced the introduction of a sweeping measure of land reform in Wyndham's 1903 Act.

Thus late-nineteenth- and early-twentieth-century Ireland no longer appears a bleak, featureless valley but something much more subtle, fragmented and open to a number of future possibilities, unlocking what Bull calls 'a new era in Irish History' [153].

PROMISING DIRECTIONS, 1900–05

Several developments converged by 1900 to suggest that the old politics of the 1880s, of nationalist pitched against Unionist, were dead and the possibility now existed for a new direction in Anglo-Irish affairs: a direction that replaced conflict with cooperation as the best path towards Irish self-rule. These developments included the reunification of the Irish Nationalist party under John Redmond, a moderate advocate of consensus politics [253]; the fragmentation of Unionism and emergence of the Russellite movement; and the investigations into a common Irish identity and cultural heritage. But of most significance for opening up a new direction in Irish politics was Wyndam's 1903 Land Act. The Act emerged from pressure by T.W. Russell's Tenant League and O'Brien's UIL, which in 1902 resulted in a land conference, composed of progressive Irish landlords, such as Lord Dunraven, and representatives of the tenant farmers, including O'Brien, Russell and Redmond. The success of the conference showed that compromise and agreement could deliver Ireland huge rewards. Lord Dunraven, in particular, worked hard to maintain the consensual spirit, forming the Irish Reform Association in September 1904, to extend agreement over land into a political arrangement based upon the devolution of certain powers to an Irish council. The Association and its proposal drew support from Sir Anthony MacDonell, Wyndham's Under-Secretary at the Castle, whose contribution had Wyndham's approval.

Cooperation between landlords and tenants, which helped produce the 1903 Act, also convinced O'Brien and Redmond that an opportunity now presented itself for 'a new policy setting forward as a future object of the Nationalist movement the conciliation of different classes in Ireland' [153 *p. 303*]. In other words, with the loss of the

Nationalist party's old *raison d'être* following removal of the land issue and with the new conciliatory atmosphere of the period 1902–04, O'Brien saw the possibility for a reinvented nationalist movement: a movement that carried *all* Irish men and women with it, regardless of class or religion and a movement that embraced the new *inclusive* Irish identities, coming from the Gaelic League and Literary Revival. Such a movement, orientated towards the conciliation of differences in Ireland, would, O'Brien believed, end the mistrust between her separate communities and give confidence that self-rule would not endanger minority rights and freedoms. This was Home Rule via consensus, something Parnell had hoped for but singularly failed to deliver, and through 1902–04 O'Brien and Redmond looked to steer the Nationalist party in this direction. This was a major development, an olive branch across the political and sectarian divide that, in part, recognised the force of Unionist fears about Home Rule: not that they cherished Westminster and Britain but they feared Nationalist 'tyranny'. 'There is as much objection to the home rulers themselves as there is to Home Rule', declared T.W. Russell [124 *p. 123*]. Remove that fear, so O'Brien thought, and a truly *all*-Irish, nationalist movement could develop, bringing solid reforms for Ireland [153].

O'Brien was partly responding to divisions within Unionism and the emergence of elements within it, such as Dunraven and perhaps Russell, who might cooperate with this line of thinking. Nor was his an over sanguinary assessment. Churchill and Carnarvon had earlier recommended a 'diluted' Home Rule plan for Ireland, while Chamberlain had offered federalism as an alternative to Gladstonian Home Rule in 1886. By 1900, most Tories on the progressive, Chamberlainite wing of the party (they would be a majority of a much-reduced party after 1906) supported some type of federal arrangement, as the logical extension to the package of constructive reforms introduced over the 1890s. Federalism was also seen as a method of satisfying growing national sentiment within an imperial framework and without weakening the British Empire as a whole, no mean consideration in an age of mounting imperial and international tension. Moreover, the contribution of Dunraven and other southern Unionist landlords in the Reform Association suggested to O'Brien that the time was ripe to strike out for a new path. Compromise was clearly in the air by 1903–04.

TURNING POINTS, 1905–09

However, the tentative attempts to build upon the conciliatory atmosphere of the early 1900s came to nothing, as the forces of traditionalism in Anglo-Irish politics reasserted themselves. This was evident within both the Nationalist and the Unionist camps. Perhaps most vociferous against the positive atmosphere were the Ulster Unionist MPs, in alliance with many right-wing Tories, who reacted 'hysterically' [124 *pp. 243–83*] to MacDonnell's involvement with Dunraven's devolution plan. This was an act of treachery by Wyndham, who they believed had been manipulated by the 'sectarian conspiracies' of MacDonnell, himself intent on introducing Home Rule by the back door, while the Tory government was at best guilty of criminal neglect and at worst passive connivance [159]. Right-wing Tories saw here a means of re-establishing control of the party against 'Chamberlainism' and its tendency to question established Tory beliefs, be it free trade or the Union. Jackson has also uncovered ulterior motives behind Ulster Unionist actions, less of hostility to Wyndham than a desire to neutralise the threat posed to their hegemony by the independent Unionist politics of T.W. Russell and Tom Sloan [124]. A 'green scare' would concentrate support back under the Ulster Unionist party. To this end the scare facilitated the creation of the Ulster Unionist Council (UUC) in March 1905, a democratically elected body aimed at limiting any future independent political activity. The UUC comprised 200 representatives from local Unionist associations and Orange clubs across Ulster, uniting rural and urban interests behind a common 'Pan-Protestantism' [16 *pp. 227–8*], that by 1907 had quietly regained control of the northern province.

As traditionalism reasserted itself amongst Unionists, so on the other side of the political divide O'Brien's 'third way' came up against the entrenched opinions of many within the nationalist movement, led at this stage by John Dillon. Dillon demanded the party keep to its 'old' methods of opposition and struggle, as he declared at Swinford [*Doc. 10*], East Mayo, in August 1903: 'having won so much by agitation in the past, we ought to press on with increased vigour until we obtain all that the country desired' [153]. He worked hard to swing party opinion his way, gaining the support of the Ancient Order of Hibernians and large sections of the Catholic Church, and importantly nationalist opinion in Ulster. Key individuals moved across to Dillon, notably Joe Devlin, MP for North Kilkenney, and Michael Davitt, the radical land reformer, though more dramatic was the drift of John Redmond away from O'Brien. Increasingly isolated, O'Brien resigned as leader of the UIL late in 1903, allowing the Nationalist party to move back towards the stance it had taken up since 1880.

Both Ulster Unionists and Nationalists, therefore, rejected the opportunities of the early 1900s, for sticking rigidly to the issues, concerns and political ritual of the 1880s. The shift towards a more conciliatory path failed to shatter the traditional mould of Irish politics. A non-sectarian, centrist political trajectory had proved an impossible plant to establish and another opportunity for Anglo-Irish relations to find a new and potentially more stable basis was lost. Indeed their relative satisfaction with the status quo sometimes brought Nationalist and Ulster Unionist into temporary alliance. In February 1905, for example, both walked through the same division lobby at Westminster on a censure motion of Wyndham. They were again on the same side in rejecting the Irish Councils Bill of 1907, part of the newly elected Liberal government's (1906–16) 'step by step' approach, which was subsequently withdrawn. And developments in Labour politics during these years would often draw opposition from both Nationalist and Irish Unionist.

Yet it was not only in the political sphere that this 'narrowing' of opportunities was evident. For in the cultural sphere there was a concomitant shift away from attempts to find a consensual and more inclusive road for Ireland. The questioning of what it meant to be Irish had led, inevitably, to disagreements. In particular the 'Irish-Ireland' movement of Moran, who regarded Catholicism and the Irish nation to be one and the same, criticised those like Yeats and the Literary Revival who put nation above religion and who advocated a more inclusive, pluralistic nationalism. For example, Irish-Irelanders charged Yeats with reinforcing the old Anglo-Irish Ascendancy, by looking back to a Gaelic past where a stable, deferential and hierarchical social system once operated harmoniously, with little reference to religion [286]: a tranquil Gaelic Ireland that united landlord and peasant, Anglo-Irish and Catholic-Irish. These differences finally came to a head after 1903 following Yeats's fiercely nationalist play *Cathleen Ni Houlihan*. The play when first shown in 1903 alarmed Catholic sensibilities by suggesting that sacrifice for Ireland stood above all other loyalties, including religious ones, an irreverence repeated more dramatically in 1907 with Synge's *Playboy of the Western World*. The play questioned the virtue of Irish Catholic womanhood, provoking riots in Dublin, which were thought to have been orchestrated by Irish-Ireland elements rather than a spontaneous outpouring of Catholic indignation, although recent historical opinion rejects this [276]. However, Yeats and the Literary Revival never recovered from the censure received in the press and especially at the hands of *The Leader*. Their brand of inclusive nationalism lost direction and sympathy within influential circles; Yeats himself even quarrelled with his partner, Maud Gonne, who later married Major

John Macbride, a fierce Catholic nationalist. With Synge's death in 1909, the most fertile period of the Literary Revival seemed over. 'The Battle of Two Civilisations', an article written by Moran about the struggle of the 1890s, appeared won by the Irish-Ireland movement [33].

In one area, however, the traditional politics of Ireland were challenged after 1905, namely the spread of more radical separatist groups [132; 155]. This was not surprising, for moves during the 1890s to eradicate the cultural influence of Britain slipped all too easily into ideas to remove the British completely. Such ideas were publicised from 1899 in the pages of *The United Irishmen* edited by W. Rooney and Arthur Griffith a journalist and Gaelic Leaguer [262]. As a result, extreme nationalist clubs emerged in the form of Dungannon clubs, Wolfe Tone memorial committees, Cumann na nGaedheal led by Griffith and, after 1906, a revived IRB movement under the dynamic Thomas Clarke, a future leader of the 1916 Rising. Overlap between the different societies, in terms of personnel and ideology, enabled them to coordinate a large campaign of protest against Edward VII's visit to Ireland in 1903, organised through a National Council [94]. The National Council folded soon afterwards, but the campaign fostered moves by Griffith and Bulmer Hobson, a militant republican and member of the Dungannon clubs, to establish a more permanent basis for their cooperation. By 1905 they formed Sinn Féin (Ourselves) as an umbrella organisation that successfully drew under it the various nationalist and republican groups.

Sinn Féin was committed to 'the re-establishment of the independence of Ireland', with a dual monarchy for Britain and Ireland, along the lines of the Austro-Hungarian Augsleich of 1867, and achieved through a policy of Irish representatives abstaining from Westminster, along the lines of O'Connell's idea of a Council of Three Hundred [26, ii *p. 157*]. They also advocated economic self-sufficiency for Ireland through a policy of protectionism. These policies distinguished them from a Fenian faith in violence to achieve Irish independence and from the Nationalist party's misplaced trust in a British electorate to grant Home Rule. But to move much beyond this was difficult for a party composed of a varied mix of individuals and opinions that included Gaelic Leaguers and literary types, members of the Irish Brigade, a group of Irishmen who fought alongside the Boers in South Africa, the American based Clan na Gael movement, romantic Irish Protestants with a love of adventure such as Sir Roger Casement and Countess Markievicz, and IRB supporters keen to infiltrate any group dedicated to removing the British from Ireland. While such a collection brought into the party a breadth of support, it unfortunately rendered agreement over policy and tactics near impossible, leaving it a weak and fragile creature. Their best election performance came at the North Leitrim by-election in February 1908, but failed to capture the seat. And despite making steady progress in local elections, the party made little headway in Irish politics before 1916. Sinn Féin was consigned, under the existing circumstances, to be 'a minority of a minority – the political offshoot of an Irish-Ireland movement' [132]. With scant funds, political in-fighting, hostility from the Catholic Church and declining support, its impact was even in full-scale retreat by early 1910, thanks largely to the return of Home Rule to the centre of British politics, which once again galvanised the Nationalist party into action.

5 CRISIS IN THE UNION, 1910–16

After nearly two decades the Irish question returned to the Westminster 'stage' with the introduction of a third Home Rule Bill in April 1912. Since it was last introduced in 1893, much had altered on both sides of the St George's channel. Ireland had undergone a social revolution, with landlords selling up and their local political power passing into the hands of the Nationalist party. In Britain, public opinion was less enthused by Irish issues, while British politicians on all sides increasingly regarded Ireland as, in the words of F.E. Smith, 'a dead quarrel for which neither the country nor the party cares a damn' [255 p. 156]. More significantly, in August 1911 a Parliament Act removed the veto powers of the House of Lords, so clearing the last major constitutional obstacle to the passage of a Home Rule Bill. All these changes suggested Home Rule now stood a real chance of reaching the statute book. But this was to ignore the Ulstermen, who organised a mass campaign of resistance, with the support of a new hardline leadership at the helm of the Conservative party. Their resistance from 1912 to 1914 went well beyond anything offered in 1886 or 1893. Together they bitterly opposed Home Rule as it advanced through Parliament, though without actually frustrating its progress. It took the outbreak of the Great War in 1914 before the government was forced to shelve its plans for Irish self-rule. Unfortunately shelving Irish aspirations provoked a small group of 'super' patriots to attempt to seize power from the British with a rising in Dublin in April 1916.

THE THIRD HOME RULE BILL AND REVOLT OF ULSTER, 1910–12

The general election of January 1910 drew Ireland back to the centre of British politics. It returned 272 Tories and 274 Liberals, leaving the balance of the House of Commons to the 82 Nationalists, a position of strength last enjoyed by Parnell in 1885–86, which had enabled him to ease Gladstone towards Home Rule. John Redmond, however, used the situation to lever the government into removing the House of Lords veto over legislation, aware, after events in 1893, that the success of any future Home Rule Bill relied on neutralising the Upper House. Asquith, the Prime Minister (1908–16), agreed, although it took a year of intense political struggle and another election in December 1910 (which simply reinforced the result of January) before a Parliament Bill was finally introduced. Its passage in August 1911 ended the Lords' power to block bills arriving from the Commons, although they could delay for three parliamentary circuits or two years. This meant that the Home Rule Bill subsequently introduced by Asquith on 11 April 1912 could become law by May 1914 at the earliest, regardless now of what the Lords did.

Asquith's bill proposed an upper house of 40 nominated senators and a lower house of 164 elected representatives. As in 1886 and 1893, the UK Parliament held ultimate supremacy over the Irish body and formal executive power still lay with the Lord Lieutenant, although everyday government would lie with an Irish Cabinet. The biggest difference between the bill of 1912 and that of 1886 and 1893 was that 42 Irish MPs were kept at Westminster, with a voice in UK affairs [106]. This emphasised that Home Rule was inimical to the separation of Britain and Ireland, and was not, as Unionists argued, conducive to it. Unfortunately for the government, Redmond rejected the idea, so allowing Unionists to claim that the Nationalists were, despite what they or the Liberals said, intent on full independence [106 *p. 75*].

Liberals approached Home Rule without the passion of 1886. Many regarded it as an administrative adjustment rather than an act of moral justice, the logical extension to government reforms of the 1890s which had transformed the economic and social basis of Ireland. In this sense they drew parallels with colonial transitions elsewhere, in Australia, New Zealand and most recently in South Africa: Home Rule was part of an exercise in imperial stock-taking that would also, and perhaps closer to their hearts, remove the Irish 'problem' once and for all from Westminster. Such arguments did little to dissuade contemporaries that government approached the enterprise with a lack of enthusiasm, its attitude being one of 'dutiful resignation' [147 *p. 184*]. The sense pervaded that it was being dragooned into it by the Nationalist hold over the parliamentary situation. As a result serious disagreements accompanied the drafting of the bill in Cabinet, with Lloyd George, Sir Edward Grey and Winston Churchill keen for some sort of separate treatment for Ulster. The bill was launched with no great popular campaign to galvanise support in the country; in fact many Liberals suspected it was deeply unpopular. And opposition attacks in Parliament and from the public platform often went unrefuted during its progress [173 *p. 53*]. Observers saw Home Rule as the product of a parliamentary bargain, though dressed up in Gladstonian moral imperatives, an impression not lost on critics who believed the government likely to 'shirk' its commitment or even 'cave-in' at the first whiff of resistance from Ulster. Nationalists, on the other hand, welcomed the bill, although they protested at certain points such as Ireland's failure to gain financial autonomy as recommended by the government finance committee. This aside, Redmond believed, as had Parnell, that Home Rule would open a new chapter in Ireland's history by reconciling her religious, social and political differences [173; 253]. The danger for Redmond was that the struggle over the bill would raise the political temperature and polarise Irish society, as it had in 1886 and 1893, making reconciliation more difficult. It was imperative that he avoid Nationalist or Catholic triumphalism and assuage, as best he could, Unionist fears of Home Rule.

Unfortunately, Redmond was unable to counter Unionist suspicions. These included a belief that Home Rule was a springboard to full separation of Ireland from Britain, and the fear that a government in Dublin, based primarily on a rural Catholic electorate, would damage the economic and industrial interests of Ireland through overtaxation or from the inevitable collapse in investment if such a government took power. Unionists also feared that their religious freedom would be endangered by a powerful connection between the Catholic Church and State. This last concern was not wholly groundless, following two papal decrees, *Ne Temere* in 1908 banning cross-denominational marriages, and *Motu Proprio* in 1911 which implied clerical immunity from civil prosecution. Drawing upon these arguments, southern Unionists, though scattered throughout the south and west of Ireland and numerically dwarfed by Nationalists, could still offer some opposition to Home Rule. They created a pressure group, the Joint Committee of Unionist Associations of Ireland (JCUAI), and exploited their influence within the British Establishment and Tory party.

But it was Unionists in Ulster who offered the greatest threat to the bill's prospects, becoming the dominant force and focus of resistance after 1910. Indeed so dominant was Ulster that historians have argued Unionism was effectively 'Ulsterised' from 1910 [124]. This view has much to recommend it. Unionism in Ulster enjoyed a far greater numerical and geographic concentration than elsewhere in Ireland, with sixteen of the eighteen Unionist MPs coming from the province. In addition they had the UUC, an organisation through which any campaign of resistance could be run. However understandable, the 'Ulsterisation' of Unionism represented a 'significant conceptual slippage' [173 *p. 22*] from an all-Ireland perspective down to a provincial one. Although Ulstermen claimed to be defending the Union as a whole, the unshakeable logic of their stance and dominance within Unionism was that in the last resort they were intent on preserving Ulster. It seemed the idea of partitioning Ireland into a nationalist south and west and a Unionist north was increasingly part of the political vocabulary, as the basis perhaps of some future compromise [186; 191]. This was an anathema to Nationalists for whom Ireland was one and indivisible, a 'seamless garment'. In deference to Redmond, Asquith ignored the separate treatment for Ulster in his 1912 bill, against the advice of Churchill and Lloyd George, but left open its inclusion at a later stage if things became too hot.

Making things hot for the government lay at the centre of Ulster's preparations to resist Home Rule, which began as early as 1910 when the bill was just a future possibility. Under the guidance of James Craig, MP for East Down, the northern Protestant community began to mobilise [258]. Orange and Ulster Unionist clubs were revived and a massive propaganda campaign was launched on the British mainland [112]. Demonstrations and marches became familiar sights, as did fierce speeches against attempts to place Ulster under a southern Parliament. Throughout the province bands of men began to drill, taking advantage of the small number of guns that were being procured with the help of F.H. Crawford, a member of the UUC's secret arms committee, and the government's relaxation of the Arms Act in 1906. Following the bill's introduction in April 1912, Unionists did all they could to upset its smooth passage through Parliament with bitter speeches, delaying amendments and various 'stunts'. Craig believed harsh words and the threat of civil disorder would mortify the government into retreat: at the very least it would undermine public support for Home Rule, so forcing the government to drop the bill or exclude Ulster from it. Once again street theatre and parliamentary 'comic-opera' were being used to advance Irish (this time Unionist) interests. To both of these tasks the arrival of Sir Edward Carson as leader of the Irish Unionists, in February 1910, was of great importance [265; 267].

Carson seemed a strange choice as leader of the Ulstermen. He was a hypochondriac, a Dubliner and MP for Trinity College, and one-time member of the National Liberal Club. He made his name at the bar, winning public recognition defending the Marquess of Queensberry against Oscar Wilde, and during the Plan of Campaign (1886–91) as Balfour's law-officer. Little in his background connected him to Ulster and initially he inspired little confidence there. Yet he soon overcame these handicaps. His strength of purpose, moral courage and a hard-hitting, no-nonsense speaking style won over a traditionally suspicious community [*Doc. 11*]. He gained a devoted following and almost cult status throughout the province, a standing Liberals and Nationalists were quick to ridicule, as King Carson the 'Prince' across the water.

Carson's real significance was as a great publicist for the interests of Ulster Unionists. He brought their concerns into the inner counsels of the Conservative leadership. His theatricality and performance as a 'stage Irishman' caught the public imagination and brought the cause of Union to the attention of British opinion. As a 'stage Irishman' he played his role to perfection. He spoke against Home Rule with passion, doggedness and sincerity, championing Ulster's right to remain under the British Parliament in the most sanguinary of terms. His large frame and long, jagged profile were the perfect anatomical accessories to his role as the hard man of Ulster. These made him easily 'marketable' [187]. A whole industry in Carson memorabilia sprang up from postcards and badges to porcelain busts. This points to the fact that propaganda was a vital element in Carson's campaign. In September 1911 he was 'presented' to the Ulster people at a huge mass meeting at Craigavon, like a 'saviour of his tribe' [183]. A year later he led the signing of the Solemn League and Covenant at the Town Hall in Belfast, a publicity bonanza in which the world's press witnessed over 250,000 Ulstermen pledge themselves to use *all means necessary* to defeat Home Rule [*Doc. 12*]. This included the threat of armed force if their concerns were not met. Carson, it seemed, had moved from upholding law and order to challenging the very basis of elected government. For here was a public declaration of rebellion every bit as treasonable and seditious as Patrick Pearse's announcement of an Irish republic from the steps of the General Post Office in Dublin at Easter 1916. Indeed, like Pearse, Carson became the conscience and moral embodiment of the people he was 'sent to save'.

We must, however, be careful not to take Carson at his word. As will become clear, he remained a nervous revolutionary, paralysed by constitutional qualms. Nor did the threats have much impact. The government remained unmoved by the extreme rhetoric, ignoring Ulster altogether when it presented its Home Rule Bill the following April. Many believed, not unreasonably, that Carson and Craig were engaged in a giant game of bluff, intent on defeating Home Rule through scaremongering and sanguinary 'froth', as Churchill called it. Instead, then, of buckling under the threat of civil commotion, the government and Nationalists preferred to deride the actions of the Ulstermen. But derision simply forced the Ulstermen to take their own words of defiance more seriously, propelling them towards even more extreme measures. Though the government chose not to notice, the situation was pregnant with danger.

What made matters worse was an almost simultaneous shift by the Conservative party leadership towards an extreme and aggressive stance against Home Rule. A tough line on Home Rule was the means by which the Tory party would escape their current political problems. By 1912 these were considerable and included three election defeats and doubts whether they would ever win again, the removal of the Lords' veto leaving no 'check' over what the radical Liberal government could do, and a dearth of fresh policies to attract public support. The way out of this mess, for the new leader Andrew Bonar Law, was to channel Tory frustrations and anxieties behind a vigorous campaign to resist the introduction of Home Rule, to the extent that Law pledged what appeared to be unlimited support for Ulster. Such an approach, he believed, would force the government to an election and on the issue of Irish Home Rule which Tories regarded as deeply unpopular in the country. At its core, then, Tory resistance between 1912 and 1914 was a political strategy aimed at returning them to office [202].

This is not to deny that they regarded Home Rule as anything but a grave danger to the unity of Empire and to national security, a hazard to property ownership and a threat to religious toleration. In addition, Tory support for Ulster was rooted in a close reading of the Constitution that held the Home Rule Bill to be illegal in the circumstances of 1912. This was because the government was forcing it into law without the scrutiny of a viable second chamber, the Lords having had their veto powers removed in August. The only way, then, to render Home Rule legal was first to put it before the people in the form of an election, which the Tories believed they could win. Of course declaring the government to be acting illegally was a dangerously open-ended conclusion, capable of justifying almost any political stratagem: if the government was acting illegally what was to limit the actions of the Tories? Although extreme in their potential consequences, Tory arguments reveal an important distinction between the Ulstermen and the Conservatives. While both wished to destroy the government and thus kill the Home Rule Bill, Tories demanded an election to achieve it. On the other hand, the Ulstermen were less eager for an election, mistrustful of the fickleness of a British electorate. Instead they sought the abandonment of the bill or, at the very least, Ulster's exclusion from it. The Ulstermen and, as we will shortly see, hardline republicans shared a common aversion to democratic accountability.

With battle-lines drawn so starkly, the struggle over Home Rule during 1911–12 was violent and bitter. In Parliament Unionists and the government clashed frequently. Unionists engaged in a full repertoire of tactics, from walk-outs and 'scenes', to a suspension of the House under threat of an all-out fray. In the country Unionists used language that had rarely been heard before or since. Both Carson and Bonar Law trod an uneasy path between bravado and sedition, and increasingly slipped over into the latter. 'It was a Gilbertian situation: the supposedly unruly Nationalist Irish were placing their trust in law and order; the staid Conservatives were inciting a province of the empire to rebellion' [195 *p. 10*].

RADICALISATION, 1913–14

And yet for all the political fireworks of 1912, Home Rule was still well on course by January 1913. The first session of Parliament had passed without loss of the bill or serious amendment, and the government's majority had held, even though Liberal backbenchers continued to show little enthusiasm. Bonar Law's solution to this failure was simply to increase his threats against the government. In January he suggested the King might refuse to grant royal assent to the bill, until an election. More dramatically Law questioned whether the British Army would obey orders to coerce Ulster under a Dublin Parliament, if called upon by the government to do so. Alongside these desperate warnings, backbench Tories, led by Willoughby de Broke and Lord Milner, established in March 1913 a British League for the Support of Ulster, aimed at helping the Ulstermen by raising money, acquiring armaments, exploiting their influence and expertise in various quarters and in the future hiring recruits [201].

Failure to move the government encouraged Ulstermen to redouble their own efforts. Early in 1913 the scattered units of men that had begun drilling in rural districts were concentrated into a single paramilitary group, the Ulster Volunteer Force (UVF), under the authority of the UUC [205]. It was organised along British Army lines, with corps, divisions and companies, and was run by retired officers, with General Richardson the Commander in Chief. In public its role was to guard the interests of Ulstermen and threaten physical resistance to the imposition of Home Rule. More privately, Ulster leaders regarded it as a useful propaganda vehicle, the focus of multiple photo-opportunities and press coverage, and as an organisation that might act as a 'safety-valve' to the growing sectarianism and militancy in the province, channelling passions into a force that could then provide control and discipline. Yet despite its enormous publicity, the UVF was never as strong as the Ulstermen claimed. Numbers were not as high or regular or as well armed as was reported, and like the Fenian movement it had a strong recreational element to it [182; 187]. It also suffered serious divisions within its leadership between politicians, military men and Belfast business interests, while central command was often in dispute with local units.

Whatever the military effectiveness of the force, historians have suggested its development marks a point of departure in the Ulster crisis when events lurched ominously towards physical-force methods as a means of solving Ireland's problems. In actual fact the UVF can be seen as a continuity in Ulster's strategy of intimidating the government into agreeing terms with Ulster; of threatening violence to secure a satisfactory political solution. For Carson and the Ulster leadership it was a political device to frighten the ministry, what Jackson refers to as 'a pliant instrument of the political leadership' [267 *p. 37*]. However, the danger was that if the UVF failed to stop Home Rule or at least win a satisfactory compromise then it would be forced, inextricably, into falling back upon its military potential: if its bark was not enough then all it had left was its bite. Carson, in other words, risked becoming a victim of his own extreme words and actions if Asquith decided not to cave in or offer a settlement. And the Conservative party, which had pledged unlimited support to Ulster through their leader, risked backing armed rebellion against an elected government. The situation resonated with danger, for all political parties, and was deepened in September 1913 when the UUC authorised the creation of a Provisional Government the moment Home Rule became law.

Militarisation by Ulster inspired the creation of other private armies in Ireland. One such force emerged during the violent Dublin lock-out of August–September 1913 that followed the strike by some 20,000 workers of the Irish Transport and General Workers Union (ITGWU) [167]. The Irish Citizens' Army (ICA), composed of some

350–400 workers, was formed by Larkin and Connolly as a 'socialist militia' to protect strikers from police brutality. The Dublin lock-out ended with little improvement in the position of the workers, but the ICA remained in existence to play an important role in later events. More significantly a Nationalist equivalent to the UVF, the Irish Volunteers, was formed in November 1913 under the leadership of the Gaelic Leaguer, Eoin MacNeill. Its intention was to prevent the government backsliding on its commitments, in the face of UVF threats, although a small number of extreme republicans and IRB men envisaged it as a force to drive the British from Ireland. Redmond was at first hostile to its formation, sensing a threat to his moderate, 'quietist' approach to the crisis. But IRB infiltration into the Volunteers and the movement's rapid growth early in 1914 forced him to seize control of it. Now, it seemed, even Redmondite constitutional nationalism was radicalising.

Asquith's answer to these dangers was to do very little. Nationalists urged him to prosecute Carson for sedition, but that would simply have added martyr status to his cult one, as it had Parnell in 1881–82. For some historians Asquith's policy of 'wait and see' in the face of such blatantly unconstitutional activity was part of a catalogue of failure. This stemmed back to his original blunder of not providing some type of separate treatment for Ulster in the original bill, through to doing nothing to prevent both sides arming themselves [189]. An alternative view of Asquith's tactics holds that his 'masterly inactivity' of tolerating the radicalisation of events was actually a method of cultivating a more 'yielding' attitude on both sides. Nothing, he believed, concentrated the mind for an eventual compromise more than the fear of civil war by all parties involved [187]. Furthermore, masterly inactivity by the Prime Minister put intense strain on the Ulster Unionist leadership. Asquith realised the growing tactical dilemma they were in, caught between a growing apprehension at the consequences of their extra-parliamentary campaign, and an expectant popular movement in Ulster, reared on a blood-curdling diet of no-surrender and with little regard for the concept of compromise. It was a movement that now required ever more extreme initiatives simply to preserve its morale and unity. Asquith's policy of 'wait and see' tweaked this dilemma, offering the real possibility of bringing the whole Ulster rebellion to a state of collapse and disunity. Of course doing nothing also raised problems for Asquith, from his backbenchers who demanded action against treasonable Unionist activity and from Nationalists alarmed by the apparent weakness of the government. In many ways the Ulster crisis had become a battle of nerves.

The full consequences of these tactical questions were, however, delayed for the moment by attempts to find a political solution before things tripped into civil war. Moderate pressure by the autumn of 1913, from the King amongst others, brought Asquith and Bonar Law together in a series of three secret meetings between October and December [189; 202]. Negotiations centred upon the exclusion of Ulster and its definition as a unit of nine, six or just four counties, and whether that exclusion was to be on a temporary or permanent basis. The talks came to nothing. Asquith was restrained by Nationalist hostility to any move away from an all-Ireland basis to Home Rule. Their case was strong. Only four counties of Ulster held a majority of Protestants, thus to ignore the wishes of the remaining 28 counties was illogical, impractical and anti-democratic. On the other side, Bonar Law wished to avoid a settlement altogether since it removed the necessity for an election. Of course his hands were tied by the Ulstermen, who looked with growing favour towards partition but could not yet go below the exclusion of all nine counties of Ulster on a permanent basis without splitting their movement. As 1914 unfolded the outlook seemed bleak indeed.

Yet things had moved on. By March 1914 the government had finally come to realise that Ulster was no longer 'bluffing' and would offer violent resistance. It therefore had a choice: appease her with concessions, a course likely to undermine Nationalist support, or coerce Ulster into Home Rule, an option liable to provoke civil unrest and undermine public support for the government, unless that coercion was made to appear legitimate. Asquith chose to face down Nationalist protest and in early March offered to exclude from the bill six counties of Ulster for a temporary period, though well aware that this was still short of what the Ulstermen 'could' accept. Unfortunately for Asquith, exploiting Unionist unreasonableness with his March offer was quickly undercut by the decision of several ministers, led by a gung-ho Churchill, to take 'precautionary measures' and reinforce military and naval installations in Ulster. The measures were little more than a series of muddled orders to be prepared for all eventualities, but to the Ulstermen, the Tory party and the press they looked like a government crackdown or as Leo Amery called it 'a plot against Ulster'. This was singularly ill-timed, for at a stroke it disabled the force and veracity of Asquith's offer. It also diverted public attention away from Bonar Law's latest ploy to force an election, by blocking the Army Annual Act in the Lords. This would have suspended the legal basis to discipline throughout the British Army, an extraordinary tactic to consider just months before the Great War

[203]. In addition, pre-emptive 'moves' against Ulster provoked an 'incident' amongst British officers at the Curragh on 20 March, 60 of whom, when offered a choice between reinforcing northern depots or 'disappearing while operations were undertaken', chose to resign their commissions [172 *pp. 1–32*]. Though not a mutiny (for they were, rather unbelievably, given a choice) and while no direct orders were disobeyed, it was a severe shock for Asquith. It now appeared the government could no longer rely on its army to crush, if need be, the rebellion in Ulster, a conclusion reinforced in April 1914 when the UVF landed 20,000 rifles, bought secretly in Germany [*Doc. 13*]. Real military force now lay behind the Ulster Provisional Government as it convened for its first sitting on 10 July.

By the summer of 1914 Ireland was sliding rapidly towards civil war. Despite a further attempt at negotiation between 21 and 23 July at Buckingham Palace, both sides remained deadlocked. Carson and Craig would go no lower than the exclusion of six counties on a *permanent* basis. Redmond, whose resolve was strengthened by a sharp increase in the size and militancy of the Irish Volunteers after their own gun-smuggling episode at Howth in late July, would not shift from exclusion on anything but a *temporary* basis. Into this stalemate came news of war on the continent. Carson and Bonar Law urged Asquith to shelve the issue for the duration of the war. The Prime Minister agreed, although he used the political accord to place Home Rule on the statute book but suspended for the war and with an amendment temporarily excluding six counties attached to it. Therefore, whereas some type of partition was probable in 1912, by 1914 it was unavoidable.

The crisis of 1912–14 had a significant impact on Anglo-Irish relations and the future direction of Irish politics. Thanks to the Ulstermen, the gun, while for a long time hovering on the margins of Irish society, was now brought decisively into it; and what 'the North began' so the south would follow [186 *pp. 45–6*]. Irish politics were militarised, a condition it would find very difficult to move away from. Ulster had been the first part of Ireland to practise 'ourselves alone', an example of independent action that would, ironically, inspire many in the nationalist movement. By their actions, Carson and Craig gained the admiration of nationalists, as Irishmen who had seized the initiative for political change from Westminster and planted it firmly in Ireland. Even Patrick Pearse could comment that 'the Orangeman with a rifle is a much less ridiculous figure than the Nationalist without a rifle' [317 *p. 185*]. In the process they revealed just how pliable a British government was to the threat of armed insurrection, observations not lost on the IRB. But more than this, the Ulster campaign of resistance acted as a baptism of fire, crafting a distinct identity for the disparate Protestants scattered throughout the nine counties of Ulster. An 'Ulster' identity had emerged that defined itself as determined, loyal and steadfast against a traitorous British government and a nationalist movement that was duplicitous and disloyal. The crisis of 1912–14 became Ulster's 'foundation moment', a baseline of aims and qualities that were used to guide and legitimate future activity [20; 187] in the same way as the Dublin Rising would for nationalists.

WAR AND THE RISING, 1914–16

On 4 August Britain went to war with Germany. According to the old Fenian dictum, 'England's difficulty was Ireland's opportunity', but for the first two years this looked improbable. War brought prosperity to the Irish economy, with swelling profits from manufacturing and the land, increased wages and the eradication of unemployment, conditions unlikely to trigger revolutionary activity. The war was also widely supported, in the early days at least, with the image of little Catholic Belgium overrun by an imperialistic Germany providing a powerful symbol for the south. As a result, and despite the IRB's attempt to stoke up opposition to the war with an anti-enlistment campaign, there was a rush to the colours that saw 50,000 Irishmen join the British Army within six months. By 1916 some 200,000 Irishmen wore a British uniform, despite recruitment falling away from 1915 onwards [181; 192]. Here in Ireland's willingness to make the ultimate test of loyalty with the supply of men for the British war-effort was compelling proof of the resilience and health of the Anglo-Irish Union. And as Ireland came to resemble an armed camp with troops either training there or on leave or awaiting passage to France, a successful rebellion seemed a very unlikely possibility. Given this environment the Irish Chief Secretary, Augustine Birrell (1907–16), acted sensibly by operating a fairly liberal regime in Ireland, in terms of the various wartime controls imposed in Britain, so preventing growth of anti-British sentiment. Redmond, keen to show the government that Ireland could be a loyal member of the Empire, pledged the Irish Volunteers to defend Ireland on behalf of the British, a call 'welcomed and applauded with enthusiasm throughout Ireland' [26, ii *p. 220*]. A month later in a speech at Woodenbridge he committed them to fight wherever the Empire needed, hoping Irish participation would reassure Unionists of Irish loyalty and, in the last resort, provide some sort of common ground that would avoid a future partition of Ireland [186]. Redmond's dominance in Ireland insured the vast majority of the Irish Volunteers (by 1914 numbering approximately 170,000) followed his call and even went as far as to rename themselves the National Volunteers. Only a small breakaway section of the Irish Volunteers rejected Redmond's line, some 10,000 at most, all with IRB connections and led by Eoin MacNeill. This was a negligible force, more concerned with uniformed parades and drilling than with creating any serious problems for the British authorities. Thus by early 1916 Ireland appeared to most observers remarkably stable: indeed just two weeks before the Rising the Director of British Military Intelligence felt the situation 'thoroughly satisfactory' [195 *p. 2*].

When, therefore, on 24 April 1916 militant republicans led by Pearse marched into the Dublin General Post Office and declared an Irish republic [*Doc. 16*], with themselves as the Provisional Government of it, the event 'came like a thunder-clap from a blue sky' [195 *p. 3*]. The rebellion took everyone by surprise, not least the nominal leaders of the Volunteers and IRB, Eoin MacNeill and Bulmer Hobson, as well as much of Dublin Castle then enjoying the bank holiday at the Fairyhouse races. Plans for a rising had evolved during 1915 amongst a tiny clique of extreme republicans sitting on the central committee of the Irish Volunteers, which included Pearse, Joseph Plunkett and Thomas MacDonagh, working in conjunction with a small military committee of the IRB led by Tom Clarke and Sean MacDermott. Details were kept from MacNeill and Hobson, who were known to be hostile to the idea of a rebellion, although the trade union leader James Connolly was brought in early in January 1916 to contain the growing friction between the Volunteers and the ICA. The Rising emerged, then, amongst a tiny clique of radical republicans, a 'conspiracy within a conspiracy' [37 *p. 196*], but wider and longer-term factors also provided the right cultural setting for it. The atmosphere of mass carnage during the Great War de-sensitised many to bloodshed and warfare: for some, like Pearse, death became an end in itself, a glorious enterprise and a noble sacrifice [*Doc. 14*]. The influence of the Gaelic League and the GAA, which had applauded ancient tales of struggle and heroic sacrifice for one's country, as with the Cuchulain story, alongside decades of Fenian mythologising of British injustice and past rebellions, played a role in shaping the mind-set of the insurgents of 1916. From this one historian has suggested that Ireland from the 1890s onwards was a 'power-keg' of frustrated nationalist ambitions, with 'the Rising ... a natural result' [184 *p. 25*].

The plan of the Rising, though never wholly clear to participants and historians alike, was to use the Easter manoeuvres of the Volunteers as cover for seizing a number of key buildings in Dublin. This would tie down the bulk of the British troops in Ireland while a wider national rising unfolded across the south and west, supplied by arms procured in Germany by Sir Roger Casement and landed on the Kerry coast. Despite some frantic last-minute confusion, the Rising began on 24 April and lasted six days. During this time much of central Dublin was brought to a standstill, with sporadic fighting between pockets of Volunteers and the British Army. The result was that much of Dublin was bombed out, with 450 people killed, 250 of whom were innocent civilians, 132 soldiers and 64 rebels [*Doc. 19*]. No national rising materialised, although there was some activity in Galway and Wexford. The Volunteer movement was broken up, with most of its recruits thrown in jail. And perhaps most depressingly for the leaders, Irish popular opinion turned to indignation, although the extent of this reaction was far from clear and according to one authority even mildly sympathetic [192]. In Dublin, the rebels faced the ignominy of being jeered by the very people they imagined they were fighting to liberate. Ironically, and in the short term at least, the outburst of violence worked to strengthen Redmond's moderate, constitutional brand of nationalism [59]. For in the aftermath the government moved quickly to broker agreement over Home Rule, with Lloyd George holding secret negotiations with both Carson and Redmond.

Militarily the Rising was a farce. The positions occupied by the rebels had limited strategic or symbolic value: few onlookers could determine why the General Post Office had been selected as the hallowed site for declaring an Irish republic, while the decision to dig and occupy trenches in St Stephen's Green when they were overlooked by near-by buildings verged on the ludicrous [206]. Volunteers were often no more than idealistic adolescents, ill-trained, badly equipped and hopelessly out-gunned. The British authorities had already intercepted the German shipment of arms on 21 April, arresting Casement (who was actually intent on *calling off* the revolt) and so destroying any prospect of a national rebellion. Those prospects were further dashed by MacNeill who, having learnt of the revolt, had cancelled the Easter manoeuvres on the day before, 23 April. This ensured widespread confusion on the morning of the Rising, with just 1,300 volunteers plus 300 ICA turning out. Whatever chance of success there had been before the seizure of the arms on the Kerry coast and MacNeill's countermanding order, now disappeared. The rebels' decision to continue with their plans 'condemned them ... to an enterprise that was doomed to disaster before it had even begun' [27 *p. 365*]. It is hard not to detect here a sense of desperation amongst the leadership, a stunt born not of widespread Irish disenchantment but a fatalistic assessment that Redmondite nationalism and indeed the British were so entrenched that no alternative existed apart from some suicidal 'epic gesture' [217 *p. 2*]

But to concentrate solely on military details is perhaps to miss the point. Some historians have argued that the Rising was intended, by Pearse, Clarke and Connolly, less to defeat the British (for in the short term that was impossible) than to shake Ireland from its torpor and regenerate a sense of national pride and destiny – a sort of patriotic 'shock-therapy' [193 *p. 48*]. For hardline republicans what Ireland needed was a very public act of sacrifice to the nation, a 'blood sacrifice' in the tradition of Cathleen Ni Houlihan. Only such an act would purify the Irish people of its Redmondite nationalism, with all its slippery compromises to British imperialism, and so provide an example and inspiration for future generations [33]. In other words the Rising was not so much a military coup as a symbolic gesture and a martyrological act, a 'foredoomed classical tragedy' performed by poets and playwrights, teachers and actors, 'to recover the literal meaning of the words Sinn Féin' [300 *p. 204*]. Of course stirring the Irish people from their 'false' consciousness of submissive loyalty to Britain implied an arrogance on behalf of the rebels that only *they* were uniquely qualified to interpret what should be the *true* consciousness of the Irish people. In their decision to stage a rebellion they showed a supreme disregard for popular or democratic accountability. Yet such objectives explain what perhaps would otherwise be unexplainable: the buildings occupied less for their military importance than their centrality to Dublin life, sure to cause maximum disruption, the choice of Easter to stage the rebellion as a symbolic time for renewal and re-birth and a determination to fight, regardless of the military imbalance; indeed its very imbalance and hopelessness were the source of its spiritual value. However, not all historians think this way. A recent and trenchant account argues that notions of a noble sacrifice were 'retrospectively relevant' and trawled from the self-exculpatory and vague writings of Pearse: at the time the IRB envisaged a full-scale war with the hope of military victory [192 *p. 25*].

Whether intentional or not, by inviting death, the Rising had a more profound impact on subsequent Irish events than if it stood (and was judged) solely on military-insurrectional terms. It helped create martyrs out of the 1916 rebels [*Doc. 17*] to the extent that the various political groups active in Irish politics after the Rising all scrambled to attach themselves to events of 1916. The Irish Labour party, for example, praised Connolly's involvement in order to legitimate their role within Irish affairs, while Sinn Féin, though hostile to the rigid republicanism of the rebels, emphasised their shared hostility to British rule and common desire for a separate Irish state. Of course creating martyrs out of inflexible republicans like Pearse created enormous problems for all subsequent Irish leaders, because to contemplate anything but a republic for Ireland was now apostasy to the creed, as enshrined in the words and deeds of the rebels of 1916. The dead, in Irish politics, would bind the living [*Doc. 18*].

The Rising also hardened differences with the Ulstermen, for whom nationalism was now irretrievably tainted as disloyal and untrustworthy [186]. This dealt a death blow to Redmond's tactical line of narrowing the gap between nationalist and Unionist, which was arguably the last chance to achieve a united Ireland through non-violent means. Such differences became all the more unbridgeable after the Somme Offensive, in July 1916, where nearly 30,000 'loyal' Ulstermen gave their own 'blood sacrifice'. Events of 1916 cemented the political divisions of Ireland, so painfully exposed by the crisis over Home Rule in 1912–14. More ominously for the future of Anglo-Irish relations, the Rising raised the profile and attractiveness of the physical-force tradition within Irish nationalism, which now emerged as a much stronger force in Irish politics.

But perhaps the most significant consequence of the Rising was the reaction it drew from the British authorities. Clearly shell-shocked by the amount of destruction in Dublin, and eager to stamp down hard on those individuals and groups at fault, the government allowed civil authority in Ireland (rule by politicians) to be replaced by military rule, so bringing Ireland under the crassly stupid leadership of General Maxwell. His understanding of restoring order consisted of the imposition of martial law throughout Ireland, mass arrests (3,500 in all, with 1,836 interned without trial at Frongoch in Wales), widespread house searches, the suppression of political groups and unsympathetic newspapers, and a host of small everyday inconveniences that slowly alienated sections of Irish society, most damagingly amongst sections who had no involvement with the Rising and who had initially shown very little sympathy for the rebel action. Such alienation was intensified by news of atrocities, from the notorious murder of Sheehy-Skeffington by a deranged British officer Captain Bowen-Colthurst, to reports of summary executions in

North King Street [176 *pp. 266–8*] and the drawn-out executions of fifteen rebel leaders. Collectively these actions set in motion a process by which Irish opinion shifted from a 'puzzled neutrality or outright hostility' to one of 'steadily more solid approval of the rebel action' [206 *pp. 27–47*]. Over the longer term this shift would prove to be politically very significant in helping to undercut the standing of Redmond and of constitutional nationalism throughout much of Ireland: his decision to condemn the Rising and 'collude with coercion' [181 *p. 63*] simply added insult to injury. There would emerge, then, a vacuum in Irish political life during the years 1916–18 that would be slowly filled by new groups, dedicated to severing the tie with Britain and willing to use whatever methods would achieve that end. In other words, the shift from Birrell's rather liberal, easy-going regime in Ireland, which understood well the complexities and delicacies of the Irish situation, to the rigid military authoritarianism of General Maxwell, marks perhaps the most disastrous policy change in the history of the Union.

6 REVOLUTION, 1916–21

Between 1916 and 1922 Anglo-Irish relations underwent a period of rapid change. Ireland moved out of the Union and towards a quasi-independent state. She agreed to become a Dominion within the British Empire, and transformed herself into the Irish Free State. This was not, however, an easy transition. Britain looked to cling hold of Ireland, engaging in widespread civil coercion and military operations to prevent her breaking away: operations that by early 1921 looked increasingly hopeless. In addition, the Ulstermen struggled to avoid assimilation into a southern Catholic assembly and to remain part of the United Kingdom. Although they failed to remain an integral part of the UK, they managed to win a separate political unit of their own, with the creation of a Northern Ireland Assembly in 1920. These last phases in the struggle to achieve Irish independence were the most dramatic, throwing up individuals and creating the myths that would dominate post-independence Ireland. Unfortunately, the most powerful myth for many within the nationalist movement was the myth of an Irish republic, which Ireland had not achieved. Independence was won, but for some, Ireland's historic objective as enshrined by the 1916 Rising had been bargained away. By 1922 those who rejected the agreement with Britain were moving against those who had accepted it and Ireland slipped inextricably and tragically into civil war.

'ALL CHANGED, CHANGED UTTERLY' (W.B. YEATS), 1916–18

As calm returned to Ireland, after Easter 1916, there was little immediately to suggest a momentous change in the political allegiance or the basis of power in Ireland. The IRB had collapsed, its leadership executed, its organisation was in turmoil and the Volunteers were in disarray. Sinn Féin, though not directly involved with the Rising, had its leaders imprisoned and its newspaper shut. Military rule operated effectively across Ireland, while in London politicians tried to recapture the political initiative by negotiating for the speedy introduction of Home Rule. The Catholic Church, alongside Irish middle-class and business interests, rejected the rebellion. A typical statement was made on 8 May 1916 by the Cork Employers' Federation, which submitted a resolution to Dublin Castle 'desiring to humbly convey to His most Gracious Majesty the King the expression of their unfailing loyalty' [230 *p. 24*]. Wider public reaction appeared confused rather than hostile to the British. The Nationalist party echoed this public mood by disapproving of the Rising but criticising military rule and demanding an immediate cessation of the executions. The legacy of the Rising was obscure. Certainly there was no obvious indication of the course events would thereafter take.

That they took such a dramatic turn after Easter 1916 owed a great deal to British policy, which managed quickly to disenchant sections of the Irish population. This set in at once with the execution of fifteen of the rebel leaders. Compared to the manner in which most European governments crushed revolts during the nineteenth and twentieth centuries, this was an extremely low level of retribution. Unfortunately, by keeping rigidly to legal form and precedent, the British authorities delayed the execution process to a long-drawn-out ten days, so allowing sympathy for the 'misguided if well-intentioned' men to grow. As a result, in straining to act within the law they simply appeared spiteful. Furthermore, by July the negotiations over the immediate introduction of Home Rule between Lloyd George, Carson and Redmond had collapsed. For many Irish it now appeared that British pledges could not be trusted and that the Nationalists were incapable of delivering on their promises or even shaping policy. These observations were reinforced by Redmond's inability to prevent the execution of Sir Roger Casement in August 1916 and Carson's re-entry into a Unionist-dominated government in December. And all the while British authority was slowly being undermined by the strong-arm, military regime of Dublin Castle. The combination of house searches, raids, control of the press, arrest of 'suspects', usually without trial, the vigorous implementation of the Defence of the Realm Act and the intelligence-gathering activities of the notorious G section of the Dublin Police Force did little to inspire Irish affection.

With no appreciable success from coercion, British policy swung early in 1917 towards a more softly-softly approach of courting Irish opinion. Prisoners taken during the Rising were released and parades in honour of the 1916 'martyrs' were legalised. Unfortunately these attempts to curry favour fell flat, as with the tumultuous reception bestowed on the returning internees and Sinn Féin's victory at the Roscommon by-election in February 1917. Worse still, British moderation sapped the morale of the RIC at what appeared to be bowing to popular pressure. Scared and somewhat at a loss, British policy swung back towards coercion from late spring 1917. After Roscommon, 31 prominent republicans were arrested on the bogus rumour that German arms were being landed [233 *p. 229*]. Sporting fixtures were prohibited, uniforms were banned and weapons could no longer be carried, while sedition and unlawful assembly were made punishable by imprisonment. In September, the Sinn Féiner Thomas Ashe died of forcible feeding by the British authorities whilst on hunger strike at Mountjoy prison. His funeral turned into a gigantic demonstration in Dublin, in a similar fashion to that of Terence Bellew MacManus in 1861 and Jeremiah O'Donovan Rossa, an old Fenian who was buried in 1915 to the accompaniment of a graveside recitation from Pearse. It seemed, therefore, that at a critical moment in Anglo-Irish relations, between 1916 and early 1918, British policy was hopelessly confused and ineffective, swinging irresolutely between the iron fist and the velvet glove: a policy 'too weak to root out opposition but provocative enough to nurture it' [246 *p. 1*]. The net result was to strengthen Sinn Féin, enabling it to consolidate its organisation and hold over sections of Irish society and to win three by-elections during the summer of 1917 at Longford, East Clare and Kilkenny.

As British authority declined so the influence of the Nationalist party began to weaken in Ireland. Redmond's power had lain in his ability to convince the British he spoke for Ireland, while simultaneously reassuring Irish supporters that he alone could win Home Rule. Unfortunately, as the British administration moved to coercion after 1916, with military rule and the failure to implement Home Rule, and as Irish opinion shifted towards a more hostile anti-British line, Redmond's strategy collapsed. When Sinn Féin won a series of by-elections during the summer of 1917, it seemed clear to all that he no longer spoke for Ireland. His loyal lieutenant Dillon urged him to take a more independent and critical line to recover support. But Redmond continued to look to Westminster, involving the Nationalist party in a British-sponsored Convention of Irish parties (which Sinn Féin and the Ulster Unionists refused to attend) to hammer out a solution. The indifference of most Irish to the Convention, and its predictable failure early in 1918, simply revealed how far opinion had moved beyond Redmond and his style of non-confrontational politics. His death in March 1918 was an eerie premonition of what would befall his party nine months hence.

This is not to argue that the rise of Sinn Féin was inevitable after 1916. For many nationalist groups sprang up or re-emerged, any one of which might have taken forward the national struggle. These included the Irish Nation League based in Ulster, the Liberty League set up by Count Plunkett, father of the executed Joe Plunkett and established after his victory at Roscommon, and the Labour party under Tom Johnson with links to Connolly's ITGWU, now under Larkin and O'Brien. In addition, the Volunteers and the IRB were re-established by Richard Mulcahy, Diarmuid O'Hegarty and a young Michael Collins, fresh out of Frongoch. Collins was already on the Supreme Council of the IRB as well as secretary to the Irish Volunteers Dependents Fund, which, like the Irish National Aid Association, was a front organisation for the IRB. Nor should we completely ignore the Nationalist party, whose influence remained strong in certain parts, notably in Ulster. Sinn Féin was just one of many political groups to appear and not the best placed to assume power, with its leadership in prison, its rejection of armed insurrection and its sympathy for monarchy.

That Sinn Féin did emerge as the leading political force in Ireland owed much to the stigmatisation of the Easter Rising as the Sinn Féin Rising, thus conveying onto them the mantle of 1916, a consecration of immense political cachet. With such a 'political kiss of life' [240 *p. 65*] the party attracted into its ranks the surviving leaders of the Rising such as Eamon de Valera, Tom Ashe and Cathal Brugha, Gaelic Leaguers and GAA enthusiasts, the National Aid Association, remnants of the Volunteer movement and IRB activists, alongside Sinn Féin's own moderate supporters. In May 1917 Sinn Féin fused with the Liberty League and established an electoral agreement with the Irish Labour party not to stand against each other at a future election. At a local level, many one-time supporters of Redmond began to move across to Sinn Féin, demoralised by his failure to win Home Rule and apparent Nationalist impotence during the Convention. Of perhaps greater significance were sections of the Catholic Church and business community who slowly gravitated towards Sinn Féin, recognising the growing irrelevance of the Nationalist party and reassured by the essential conservatism of many within the movement on economic, social and religious matters, notably Griffith and de Valera.

By October 1917, and despite the best efforts of the British authorities, Sinn Féin had 1,200 clubs and nearly 66,000 members, a staggering increase from just 11,000 at the start of 1917. But rapid growth altered the composition and values of the party. Sinn Féin now held a wide and unstable mix of political beliefs, and resembled little more than an umbrella organisation or 'flag of convenience' [240 *p. 67*]. Advocates of physical-force methods lined up besides supporters of the constitutional path to Irish freedom. And republicans nestled uneasily with monarchists, socialists, radical agrarians and Home Rulers, each believing their politics was the goal towards which the movement should work. In such circumstances unity was impossible but cooperation was preserved around a basic platform of separation from Britain and abstention from Westminster, although what was meant by separation was left suitably vague. To have clarified policy further would have split the organisation.

Yet if Sinn Féin were to become a serious political force some form of policy stance and common platform was required. This was achieved in October 1917 at the party conference (*ard fheis*) where a working relationship was agreed around the formula [*Doc. 20*]: 'Sinn Féin aims at securing the international recognition of Ireland as an independent Irish Republic. Having achieved that status the Irish people may by referendum *freely choose* their own form of Government' [2 *p. 514*]. There was something here for everyone. Republicans did not look beyond the first sentence, believing fervently in an Irish republic which the people had no right to dismantle once founded. For them, sovereignty lay in Pearse's 1916 Proclamation (and thus the IRB Supreme Council which now exercised that sovereign power), not with the easily misguided Irish populace described by Liam Lynch, a future IRA commandant, as 'sheep to be driven anywhere at will' [224 *p. 43*]. The physical-force men of the IRB went along with the compromise as far as it suited their immediate purposes but few had time for political niceties or had relinquished their commitment to armed insurrection: in the words of one of their leaders, 'we just listened to all the orations and prognostications and made up our own mind' [308 *p. 48*]. On the other hand moderates, who were not so rigidly tied to militant republicanism, looked to international opinion rather than armed force to win Irish independence. They were reassured that the people, whom they believed to be deeply conservative, had the ultimate sanction to choose freely for Ireland whatever form of government they desired. Much, then, was left purposely vague and the compromise formula had the air of a delaying mechanism rather than a solution. But in the difficult circumstances of 1917, a working agreement linking the various wings and traditions of the nationalist movement allowed Sinn Féin to move forward. The compromise was given immediate force by Griffith's resignation as President of Sinn Féin in favour of de Valera, a post he now combined with President of the Volunteers, so 'combining under one man the military and political wings of the nationalist movement' [271 *p. 70*].

But for all the advance made by Sinn Féin during 1917 and early 1918, its political impact would have remained marginal if not for the British decision to extend conscription to Ireland on 9 April 1918, a move Lloyd George's government tried to sweeten with the promise of another Home Rule Bill. The decision was rooted in Britain's severe manpower shortages and as a political sop to the Tories and Unionists who dominated the coalition ministry. However, almost at a stroke it radicalised the situation. Irish reaction was uniformly hostile, and Sinn Féin exploited this. Drawing on its current popularity and growing local organisation, it launched a campaign of mass resistance that drew in the wider nationalist community, including trade unions, the churches and even sections of the Nationalist party. On 18 April at Dublin's Mansion House this pan-nationalist alliance agreed to resist the imposition of conscription 'by the most effective means possible': a development and form of words that echo the Ulstermen's Solemn League and Covenant of 1912 [*Doc. 21*]. A National Defence Fund was established with local committees in the towns and villages, many of which were organised by the IRB, ever hopeful of turning events towards another military confrontation against the British. More dramatically, the trade union movement responded with a one-day general strike on 23 April that brought much of Ireland, outside Ulster, to a standstill [230 *pp. 33–8*].

The campaign against conscription and the general strike met with a predictable response from the British. Lord French, the new Lord Lieutenant who had been given extra powers by the government, used the cover of a 'German plot' to arrest the Sinn Féin leadership. He followed this up with internment of 'suspects' and banning any group connected with the party, including the Volunteers and Gaelic League. In June he went further and 'proclaimed' Kerry, followed by West Cork in September. The result of these actions was to drive what remained of the Sinn Féin organisation underground, from where it became tighter, more efficient and less easy to monitor. Sinn Féin membership rose during 1918 to 112,000 and its popularity was reflected in the election of Arthur Griffith as MP for East Cavan, despite languishing in an English prison. British repression worked to bolster the standing of Sinn Féin just months before Ireland went to the polls at the 1918 general election. More worryingly, with much of its political leadership in prison, control of the movement passed to the IRB and Volunteers, and in particular to Collins and Mulcahy, who had evaded arrest. Thanks to heavy-handedness from Dublin

Castle, as the Great War neared its end the struggle for Irish independence lay firmly with men dedicated to active military resistance to British rule.

THE GENERAL ELECTION AND RISE OF A COUNTER-STATE, 1918-20

At first this shift within the Sinn Féin movement was not clear, as constitutional politics revived with the announcement of a general election for November 1918. This was the first election since 1910 and was held in very different circumstances. A Redistribution and Franchise Act had altered many of the electoral boundaries in Ireland while nearly trebling the electorate, now composed of many young impressionable first-time voters whose political horizons had been shaped by a variety of events that included the pre-war crisis over Ulster, the Rising, the British counter-reaction after 1916, and above all else the threat of conscription. When the result of the general election came through it confirmed the direction Irish politics had taken since 1912 and especially since 1916. Sinn Féin won 73 seats and the Ulster Unionists gained 26, an increase of 10 on their 1910 share. Partition, always likely since 1912, now looked unavoidable [186]. But as dramatic was the collapse of the Nationalist party from a pre-election 78 seats to just six, most of which were in the constituencies bordering Ulster. Here in the results of 1918 was an electoral revolution that gave Sinn Féin a popular mandate for change and made some form of revision of the Act of Union inevitable, although the British still chose to ignore it.

On closer inspection the result was less startling. The discrepancy in seats owed something to the widespread intimidation of voters and impersonation by the IRB and GAA: it was clear 'the dead had voted in large numbers' [265]. In addition election boxes were 'stuffed' and votes went 'astray', to an extent that Garvin refers to the election as 'a doubtful expression of the popular will' [224 *p. 38*]. Labour's decision not to stand candidates in the election, having reached a prior agreement with Sinn Féin, gave the latter a free run in many constituencies. Similarly the Nationalist party failed to contest every seat. These developments, as well as the workings of the British first-past-the-post system, enabled Sinn Féin to win 70 per cent of the seats on just 48 per cent of the vote, whereas other non-republican Nationalists won nearly 25 per cent of the vote for just 5 per cent of the seats. It is also conceivable that much of Sinn Féin's support represented a rejection of the old Redmondite party rather than sanction for republicanism or a glowing endorsement for Sinn Féin and its objectives. Few understood what Sinn Féin stood for, a vagueness that probably helped its unity and electoral appeal.

What all Sinn Féiners did agree on was abstention from Westminster and the formation of an Irish Constituent Assembly. On 21 January 1919 the Sinn Féin MPs publicly convened themselves as an independent Parliament for Ireland, the Dáil Éireann. Its first act was to ratify documents drawn up in a series of party meetings between 2 and 19 January. These included a new Constitution, a Declaration of Independence and more controversially a commitment to a Democratic Programme, introduced largely to preserve relations with the growing Labour movement [235 *pp. 10–22*]. This promised to improve the living of all Irish people through an extension of state responsibility. The inaugural meeting of the Dáil was largely a propaganda gesture, more reminiscent of a Sinn Féin Convention than a national constituent assembly. The fact that only 27 members attended the 'historic' first meeting, with 34 held in English jails, eight absent and all Unionists and constitutional Nationalists refusing to attend, impaired its legitimacy. Like the rebels of 1916, the Dáil's claims to represent the Irish Nation were balanced upon narrow and exclusionist foundations. Indeed there were twice as many foreign journalists as Irish representatives present, pointing to the key role publicity would play in Sinn Féin's strategy for ridding Ireland of the British.

In this the various conferences at the end of the war were an ideal forum for publicising the Dáil's claim to represent Ireland. In February 1919 Irish Labour leaders were granted a seat at the Socialist Convention in Berne. A more ideal stage to seek recognition, and one to which the Dáil appealed for support on 21 January, was the Peace Conference at Paris. Here, under the influence of President Wilson's Fourteen Points, Irish representatives struggled to gain international acknowledgment for Ireland's independent status, posing (not unfairly) as another small nation liberating itself from the debris of an old European empire. Unfortunately Sean O'Kelly, the Irish representative, failed to win recognition at Paris. Britain's was the one European empire not to have collapsed and none of the victorious powers, especially the USA, were going to alienate her at such a moment. And after June 1919 the opportunity was lost with the signing of the Paris settlement. Irish representatives had better luck in the United States where both the Senate and House of Representatives passed resolutions urging the Paris Conference to consider Irish claims and a delegation of Irish-Americans from the Irish Race Convention gained access to Wilson. Later they visited Ireland, to be greeted by the Dáil as an 'official' US representative mission and winning extensive press coverage in Britain. The American connection was to be (and to some extent had always been) the vital arm of Ireland's struggle, in terms of world publicity, money, arms and men. The central importance of America explains why Eamon de Valera, recently escaped from Lincoln Jail and made President of the Irish Republic in April 1919, spent nearly eighteen months in the States between June 1919 and December 1920.

Despite some success in the United States it was clear by early 1920 that international recognition had not been won by the Dáil. As a result it increasingly concentrated its efforts upon constructing a viable 'counter-state'. This was a strategy deeply embedded in Sinn Féin philosophy and with Griffith especially, who believed the best way to 'achieve self government was simply *by practising it*' [235 *p. 50*]. Accordingly the Dáil began to build the institutions of a modern state. In April 1919 a Cabinet was elected by the Dáil. Alongside de Valera as President were Griffith at Home Affairs (and acting President during de Valera's absence in the USA), Cathal Brugha at Defence, Count Plunkett at Foreign Affairs, William Cosgrave at Local Government and Michael Collins at Finance, a post he combined with those of Director of Intelligence and President of the Supreme Council of the IRB. From this executive head mushroomed a variety of government committees and bodies that sought to replace British authority and control. These included law and order, local courts of justice, commissions for the land, fishing, forestry, trade, banking, finance, cooperatives and education. In addition a Commission of Inquiry was established to investigate the resources and industries of Ireland. Once again propaganda was one of the prime motives behind these developments, for to be 'seen' to challenge British rule gave credibility to the enterprise. Of course the reality of that challenge often left a great deal to be desired, inhibited as it was by a lack of finance, increased harassment from Dublin Castle, particularly after the Dáil was declared illegal on 11 September 1919, a lack of experience by the young revolutionaries suddenly thrust into administrative roles, poor communications and the imprisonment of many of their representatives. In March 1920, for example, only nine members of the Dáil remained outside prison or on the run, six of whom were out of Ireland. As a result, the Dáil met very infrequently; large stretches of the period 1919–21 saw little if any activity at Dublin centre. Therefore the achievement of the Dáil in establishing a viable counter-state was, for one historian, 'questionable – a matter for propaganda and later historians keen to simplify a muddled situation' [228 *p. 7*].

This probably pushes things too far. For Mitchell, the Dáil counter-state was undoubtedly limited and chaotic, but worked. A network of couriers maintained links between the various parts of government in a system he describes as 'government by bicycle' [235 *p. 55*]. Even though the Dáil as a whole met infrequently, much of its business was carried out by a host of groups and bodies from a variety of different premises scattered around Dublin. Through a Loan Scheme, launched in spring 1919, as well as the steady influx of money from the USA, substantial funds were available to effect a form of 'make-shift' government. And whether viable or not, the Dáil Eireann 'was now seen by many, if not most, people as the de facto government of the country' [235 *p. 154*]. British administration was being eaten away from within.

But to concentrate on activities at the centre is to misread the nature of events in Ireland during this period. In many areas the initiative for change came from the locality. For example, local republican courts began to establish themselves from late 1919, in response to the retreat of the Royal Irish Constabulary (RIC) from the Irish countryside as a result of mounting attacks from the Irish Republican Army (IRA) and the subsequent breakdown in law and order. Though muddled and little more than *ad hoc* committees (they would often meet at the local bar or hotel), these 'alternative' courts were able to provide a workable system of law, presided over by a priest or lawyer and backed up by the IRA to administer punishment. The Dáil gave retrospective sanction in June 1920 by assuming judicial responsibility, but the system was already working well, gaining support from local communities and from the Irish legal establishment. Land was another area the Dáil was forced to intervene in by local developments. The upsurge of rural violence early in 1920, with the eruption of land agitations, attacks on graziers, cattle drives and seizures of land, a consequence of the collapse in law and order, raised anxieties amongst tenant farmers and middle-class Catholics for the safety of their property [209]. The Dáil, aware of the comparisons being drawn in parts of the press between 'Sinn Féinism' and Bolshevism, were keen to reassure this powerful and conservative constituency. They therefore established land courts to arbitrate disputes, a Land Commission to continue the work of redistributing the land, and a National Land Bank to facilitate the exchange. Again the IRA acted as the unofficial 'policeman' in rural areas, preventing land seizures and maintaining order far more effectively than the RIC was able to do. These initiatives from the locality were strengthened in March 1920 when Sinn Féin fought the local government elections, winning 560 of the 1,816 seats across Ireland. Its involvement was designed as a propaganda exercise to reiterate to the British government its continued popularity; as with the elections to Westminster, its intention was abstention. However, the scale of the Dáil's victory, as well as renewed fears of middle-class disenchantment at the possible breakdown of local services, forced it into assuming control of the British established structure of local government.

Thus by 1920 the Sinn Féin counter-state had put down deep institutional roots throughout Ireland. It won mass popular support, though not in parts of Ulster where the Ulstermen were busy building up their own counter-state. Most important for its survival, it attracted support from the Church and from the professional classes. But its success owed a great deal to the space opened up in Irish society by the decline of British authority and power, for which the Dáil's military campaign was largely responsible.

ANGLO-IRISH WAR, 1919–21

Under the threat of conscription and with widespread British repression, a renewed military campaign by what remained of the IRB and Volunteers began to develop. The return of republican prisoners in 1917, whose time at Frongoch had been used to learn guerrilla tactics and establish contacts, and the subsequent imprisonment of the political leadership of Sinn Féin, gave added impetus to the military option. It has also been suggested that the drift in Ireland towards a military engagement stemmed from an excess of young men, eager for military glory and conditioned to bloodshed. This was the result of restrictions placed on emigration from Ireland during the war years, so creating a reservoir of new recruits. But it was also the product of a traditional gang-culture in rural Ireland [222], in which many young Irish men involved themselves and were recently strengthened by the comradeship and 'male solidarities' that developed during the war [224 *p. 41*]. Thus rather than just one or two boys from a village joining the Volunteers, the young men from a whole community would.

The Dáil had very little control over this emerging military initiative, and even the Oath of Allegiance which all Volunteers were forced to swear to the Dáil in August 1919 did little to restrain local commanders. This reflected a basic division within the Dáil and the Sinn Féin movement as a whole, between those of a political mentality, such as Griffith, de Valera and Cosgrave, and those of a military one, such as Collins, Mulcahy, Tom Barry and Dan Breen. The latter 'type' gloried in activism and independent action as the way to win Irish freedom and despised the 'flag-wagging, speech-making and parading organisation ... and harmless pursuits' of the 'politicians' [307 *p. 60*]. In other words the heterogeneous nature of Sinn Féin, under whose umbrella a variety of extreme nationalist, revolutionary and republican groups sheltered uneasily, prevented it from ever fully coalescing around a common aim or strategy or from allowing the leadership to establish control [*Doc. 23*]. Lack of central direction over the military campaign reflected the complex and localised evolution of what became known by 1919 as the IRA. This was a loosely organised body composed of the remnants of the Volunteers, the IRB, various defence or athletic groups and traditional agrarian secret societies. Unfortunately, authority over and within these groups remained highly confused and contested, often being based upon personality or local standing. By mid-1919 Collins had come to exert a powerful influence across the various strands that made up the IRA, largely through force of character and a huge capacity for detailed work; 'the 'big fella' was 'everything', declared one IRA commander [228 *p. 6*], even though he was formally subordinate to Brugha, as Defence Minister and Mulcahy as IRA Chief of Staff.

Moves towards a military engagement with the British began slowly and under the direction of local Volunteer groups, the first shots being the murder of two policemen at Soloheadbeg on the very day, 21 January 1919, the Dáil was convened in Dublin [223]. This was an eerie but not accidental juxtaposition of the military and political paths to Irish freedom. The attack embodied the essence of IRA methods and objectives up to 1921. It was carried out by local activists, using guerrilla tactics, as a consequence of limited men and arms, and on their own initiative, without orders from high command; indeed their aim was probably to force their central leadership into a more ruthless, military campaign against the British. Secondly, the Soloheadbeg volunteers attacked the RIC. Assaults on the police, especially those in isolated rural barracks, would be the mainstay of IRA activities with the intention of rendering Ireland ungovernable. In addition attacking the police would be a highly 'provocative' act, sure to ellicit an aggressive response from the British, 'with the result that such state activity would alienate large sections of the population' [217 *p. 50*]. This would then 'legitimate' reprisals by the IRA which, in turn, would be met by counter-reprisals from the British. Thus a ratchet-like spiral of violence would be set in motion, undermining British authority amongst local people and sapping the will of the

British authorities to continue in what Hart has called the 'runaway tit-for-tat logic of guerrilla war' [227 *p. 17*].

Like any guerrilla force, the IRA became adept exponents of ambushes, assassination, 'disappearances', the execution of informers, the sabotage of enemy communications and the intimidation of local communities against helping or even consorting with the enemy. Alongside these methods of disrupting British rule they used the traditional Fenian method of protest, the hunger strike, as a means of publicising their claims and winning support for their cause. The most famous example of this was the death of the Lord Mayor of Cork, Terence MacSwiney, on 25 October 1920, after 74 days of hunger strike in Brixton prison. But the IRA also developed new techniques of resistance. For example, the emergence of the Flying Column. These were small bands of men 'on the run' and living off the land, who were highly mobile and could quickly form into a large unit to ambush the enemy, before melting back into the countryside and hills.

Yet perhaps the greatest ally of the IRA was the British authorities. Their response to attacks on outlying police stations and to the fall of recruitment into the RIC was to hire ex-British soldiers into two new 'elite' units, the Black and Tans, to augment the police, and to use ex-officers, the Auxiliaries, to engage the IRA directly. These groups, which Margery Forester memorably refers to as 'the sediment of a heavily populated country' [264 *p. 136*], responded in kind to IRA activities. They engaged in wholesale violence, theft, drunken rampages, attacks on villages such as the burning of Balbriggan in August 1920, and the murder of suspects or 'Shinners', sometimes on the flimsiest of evidence or for simply being in the wrong place at the wrong time [*Doc. 22*]. This played directly into the IRA's hands, 'a boomerang against those who had cast it' according to Dan Breen, leader of the Tipperary IRA, and began a cycle of reprisal and counter-reprisal [308 *p. 104*].

The low point in this 'tit-for-tat' conflict came in the autumn and winter of 1920. It was sparked by the execution of Kevin Barry, a young Volunteer and the first execution since 1916, and the murder of an IRA man John Lynch by a notorious group of British intelligence officers known as the Cairo Gang. Collins, aware of the pressure British intelligence was placing upon the IRA at the time, replied with a military-style execution of fourteen British agents in Dublin, early on Sunday 21 November 1920. In reaction, Auxiliaries and Tans broke up a football match at Dublin's Croke Park that same afternoon where they carried out 'diabolical reprisals', machine-gunning dead fifteen people in the crowd. This incident, long remembered as Bloody Sunday, fuelled the popular myth of Collins as a brilliant, if necessarily ruthless, guerrilla leader and the British forces as brutal and indiscriminate in their violence. Yet, according to one authority, the shooting of fourteen intelligence men was more the result of 'slackness and indiscipline' by the Auxiliaries, than exceptional cunning and guile by Collins's squad [246 *pp. 129–31*]. And events later that day in Croke Park were the consequence of a stampede; more people died from being crushed than from being shot. Undoubtedly Auxiliaries shot into the crowd, but not with machine-guns (there surely would have been many more casualties) and, it seems probable, in response to IRA shots. Reprisals were after all a central aspect of IRA strategy. A week later the West Cork Brigade of the IRA, led by Tom Barry, ambushed a detachment of Auxiliaries at Kilmichael in West Cork, killing sixteen, some in cold blood after they had surrendered [227 *pp. 21–38*], to which the Tans replied by 'sacking' Cork town.

These were the dramatic 'headline' events in what was, in actuality, little more than a dirty war between small groups of hard men and gangsters on both sides – men who were incapable of readjusting to the normalcies of peace after the bloodletting of the previous five years. It was a conflict characterised by spies and informers, of midnight executions and a bullet in the back of the head, of guilt by association or family or religion, and of widespread intimidation of the local populace by both sides. Yet, as became increasingly apparent, it was a war neither side could win. As the reality of this sunk in by the summer of 1921, so the British moved haltingly towards a truce, finally agreed on 11 July, and opening the way to more formal peace negotiations.

'A TRICK OF ENGLISH POLITICIANS' (DE VALERA): HOME RULE FOR THE NORTH, 1919–21

Since 1885, and particularly between 1912 and 1914, a distinct Ulster Unionist identity had emerged amongst Protestants in the north-east of Ireland – an identity constructed around defence of the Union with Britain and loyalty to the Crown, and defining itself against a disloyal, separatist, Catholic Irish majority [186 *pp. 1–43*]. These sentiments had been confirmed by the Rising of 1916 and the huge campaign against conscription in May 1918, which represented, for the Ulstermen, acts of disloyalty that reinforced their desire to remain outside any future southern-dominated Parliament. Yet equally they could never trust a British government not to sell them short and place them under an all-Ireland government, as seemed likely during the Home Rule crisis of 1912–14 and the Irish Convention of 1917. This fear, though ever-present during these years, was diminished by the general election of 1918. Here Ulstermen strengthened their position. They acquired 26 MPs, who, because of the withdrawal of Sinn Féin MPs from Parliament, now enjoyed unrivalled influence over Irish policy. This they used to press hard for a secure political home, which for many still meant rule from Westminster, or as a lesser option the partition of Ireland into nationalist and Unionist blocks, each with their own separate 'devolved' assembly.

From 1919 control of government policy for Ireland resided in the Irish Committee, under Walter Long, charged with formulating an alternative to Asquith's suspended Home Rule Bill of 1914 [270]. The thinking of Long at this time ran towards some form of Home Rule for both north and south, a solution that embraced the partition of Ireland. This had much to recommend it. It was a quick-fix solution, acceptable to the Ulstermen, though not to the absent Sinn Féiners, who rejected any scheme that divided Ireland. In the eyes of the United States and Dominion territories it was a fair settlement, not least because it took Britain out of Ireland, giving the Irish people a large measure of control over their affairs. The only uncertainty was where to make the cut. One plan was to establish a northern Parliament out of four counties of Ulster (Antrim, Armagh, Derry and Down). This corresponded to the demographic concentration of Protestants and to Unionist parliamentary representation, and would probably have been the outcome if all nine Ulster counties were given a plebiscite on their future. But four counties was thought to be 'administratively unworkable' and for this reason lacked support from the Ulstermen, aware of how weak such a structure would be [213; 214]. Nor did the Ulstermen favour a Parliament of all nine Ulster counties, since it would include those with a clear Catholic majority (Donegal, Cavan and Monaghan), and those with a slight Catholic majority (Fermanagh and Tyrone). As a result such an arrangement would, in the words of Sir James Craig, leader of the Ulstermen, so 'reduce our majority to such a level that no sane man would undertake to carry on a Parliament with it' [24 *p.* 6], thus leaving the 'statelet' vulnerable to a future Catholic take-over and re-unification with the south. Craig pushed instead for a six-county solution (the Protestant-dominated four counties plus Fermanagh and Tyrone) as the safest and most defendable unit. This, however, would have left a large number of northern nationalists, about one-third of its population, under the domination of Ulster Unionists (just as some

200,000 southern Unionists would be left under the southern Irish State). But the government ignored their protests and accepted the Ulstermen's preference by introducing a Government of Ireland Bill that partitioned Ireland into a 26-county south and a six-county north, both with a Home Rule Parliament. As a sweetener to the nationalists, they included a Council of All-Ireland to undertake matters of common concern, such as fishing. But this was ignored by the Ulstermen and fell into disuse. The bill passed into law in December 1920 with elections to the new assemblies held in May, at which Unionists swept 40 of the 52 seats in the northern Parliament. In the south, Sinn Féin participated simply to reinforce its popular mandate, winning 124 of the 128 seats and convening not as the southern Home Rule Parliament but as the second Dáil. Once again a British-sponsored election served to reinforce Sinn Féin's hold over the people of Ireland.

The Northern Ireland Assembly set about constructing its own state apparatus, with Craig appointed Prime Minister and head of the government. But its position was anything but secure. From August 1920 it faced economic boycott by the Dáil and an IRA campaign aimed at destabilising it, with the 'moral' support of many northern Catholics who still hoped for unity with the south [245]. In addition, and despite pledges from Lloyd George to the contrary, the fear persisted amongst Ulstermen that the political arrangement was not permanent and might be further revised or even dissolved, if the exigencies of British politics so demanded. And if dissolved, then there was sufficent evidence from IRA activities against Protestants and Unionists in the south about how a Catholic-dominated government in Dublin would treat them. Such threats reinforced Ulster's siege mentality: for northern Protestants, surrounded by enemies and threatened within by 'disloyal' elements, the moment bristled with deep historic meaning of ancient battles and die-hard resistance. To 'defend the statelet' [24 *p. 15*] from IRA attacks, a new Ulster Special Constabulary was formed from remnants of the UVF and other loyalist paramilitary groups. Unfortunately, in the tense atmosphere of 1920–21, defence quickly spilled over into widespread sectarian attacks on Catholics, particularly from the part-time contingent of the Constabulary, the so-called B Specials. Sectarianism also took legal form with the imposition of controls upon the Catholic communities, such as the Special Powers Act granting the Constabulary almost unlimited power and the Local Government Emergency Powers Act of 1921 that allowed the Northern Ireland government to dissolve any locally elected council and remove Catholics from positions of power.

By 1922, it appeared the defence of 'Ulster's' way of life was being won at the expense of denying Catholic freedoms and liberties, the very grounds upon which Unionists had resisted incorporation under a Dublin Parliament.

BRITISH POLICY IN IRELAND, 1919–21

Since 1916, British policy in Ireland had alternated between moderation and coercion, a traditional combination that progressively alienated sections of the Irish population, demoralised the RIC and revealed confusion and drift at the heart of the Irish administration. This continued into the peace. The new Chief Secretary, J. MacPherson, was eager to pursue a more softly-softly 'political' line in order to win over moderate Irish opinion. As such his administration greeted the creation of the Dáil in January 1919 not with coercion but with an embarrassed nonchalance; repression at this point, it was felt, would only breathe life into the infant assembly and in any case many believed it would quickly fall apart. In March prisoners were released to alter the balance of Sinn Féin away from the 'fire-eating' military men. And attempts to open negotiations with Sinn Féin were made during a secret visit to Ireland by Lord Haldane early in 1919. These initiatives, however, came to nothing and in the circumstances of 1919 it was difficult to see how or where a political solution could emerge. On the one hand stood a powerful and resolute Sinn Féin publicly committed to an Irish republic; on the other stood the British government, determined to move no further than Home Rule and to re-establish its authority over Ireland, aware of the dangers of imperial fragmentation if Ireland were allowed to float free. All the while, IRA attacks against the RIC continued to escalate, strengthening the hand of those groups at Dublin Castle, centred around the Viceroy, Lord French, with the support in London of hardline imperialists such as Lord Milner, Lord Curzon and Winston Churchill, who advocated a tougher approach.

The daylight assassination of an RIC District Inspector in Thurles on 23 June 1919 shocked moderate opinion at Dublin Castle and gave French the excuse to inaugurate a more coercive regime. Meetings and assemblies were prohibited. On 4 July Sinn Féin was 'proclaimed' illegal in Tipperary, later extended across the whole of Ireland, along with bans on the Gaelic League and Cumann na mBan, the female auxiliary section founded by Constance Markievicz. To restore RIC morale, pay and conditions were improved and a scheme of fortifying barracks introduced. An IRA attack at Fermoy on 7

September provided further justification for declaring the Dáil illegal, although the actual cause had much to do with Dublin Castle's growing fear that a viable counter-state was being successfully constructed under their noses. By late 1919 British policy had shifted towards coercion, driven by a failure to find common cause with moderates in Ireland and, to a larger extent, by an intensification in the IRA's campaign, itself designed to draw the British into a wider 'military' engagement.

The attempted assassination of Lord French, in December 1919, helped transform the existing policy of still 'mild coercion' [246 *p. 1*] into full-scale Cromwellianism. Sir Hamar Greenwood replaced MacPherson as Chief Secretary, Sir Nevill Macready took charge of the army and General Tudor became Chief of Police. Their first acts were to expand the intelligence service in Ireland and begin the paramilitarisation of the RIC. This was achieved by recruiting de-mobbed British soldiers into new units to operate alongside the RIC, the Black and Tans and the Auxiliaries, on the assumption that the 'RIC had to become military to survive' [246 *p. 40*]. Government was keen to keep 'the Irish job ... a Policeman's job', for to use the army was to admit it was a war in Ireland and their enemy not rebels but soldiers in defence of their land (echoes of this would again be heard during the hunger strikes of the 1980s). With little discipline or self-control, these 'elite' units formed 'a counter-murder association' [260 *p. 165*], implementing reprisal, execution, retaliation and summary punishments, with an unofficial 'nod and wink' from the British government. 'We have murder by the throat', Lloyd George declared some months later [*Doc. 22*].

Nothing was further from the truth. The introduction of a 'foreign' military element and ethos into the police destroyed whatever link and respect survived between the local community and the RIC. It created a basic confusion within the forces of law and order: were they an army acting like policemen, or policemen acting like an army? Failure to solve this led to disagreement and muddle at all levels of the British administration. The result of Tan 'atrocities' was to strengthen IRA activities by providing them with support from the local community. Nor did the continuity of wartime government powers, with the Restoration of Order Act of August 1920, or the application of martial law to eight counties by December, bring a halt to IRA activities. Indeed by early 1921 those activities had brought about the near total incapacitation of civil government in Ireland. Here was a conflict the British could not win in any military sense, unless they were willing to flood Ireland with troops and impose full-blown terror tactics, and even then 'to make a desert and call it peace was in no sense a solution' [234 *p. 249*]. In addition, violence and reprisal had raised loud protests from the USA and Dominions, and drew an increasingly hostile response from British public opinion, stoked by the Peace for Ireland Council. Against this background, and facing the awful prospect of imposing Crown Colony status onto the south for refusing to cooperate with the 1920 Government of Ireland Act, moves towards a truce began early in 1921. Terms were finally agreed between the British and Sinn Féin in July following a conciliatory speech from George V.

Squeezing the British to a truce has been represented as a military victory for the IRA, with the 'war of independence' a heroic struggle, won against the vastly superior forces of the British Empire. On balance, events were much less spectacular. The war had been little more than a series of limited engagements, declining in frequency by late 1920 as the RIC moved into secure urban barracks, and interspersed with long periods of inactivity. Most Irish people, on both sides, were appalled at the violence, practising a 'studied neutrality, keeping their heads down and praying for peace' [224 *p. 73*]. Accordingly, the geographic spread of IRA activity was very narrow, concentrated around Dublin and in Munster province, with only sketchy recruitment in the west or from the rich agricultural counties of the centre and east. 'It was a localised entity, with pockets of complete dedication, a few centres of reliable support and areas where there was hardly any organisation' [207 *p. 39*]. Nor did the IRA defeat the British; the most one might say is that a military stalemate was reached between two exhausted sides. And not before time, for by the spring of 1921 the IRA was near collapse, with an acute lack of ammunition, the loss of hardened guerrilla fighters after the disastrous attack on the Custom House in May 1921, and from fractures within the movement itself [*Doc. 23*]. Tensions occurred at all levels of the republican movement, between the political and military leadership, between central command in Dublin and local IRA leaders 'in the field', and even between different regional IRA units. Moreover, as the military campaign grew so the IRA became embroiled in a host of local rivalries, family feuds, individual disputes, especially over land, as well as criminal activity where Volunteers used the breakdown in law and order to profit. Ideological strains also sapped the unity of the movement [217]. Die-hard republicans fought for an Irish republic and would settle for nothing less. Yet republican socialists saw true Irish freedom only reached through economic transformation and redistribution of the land, forming links with Labour and encouraging land seizures and cattle drives. Sinn Féin moved quickly to halt these developments, eager not to lose the support of the Catholic Church and the middle classes: theirs was a nationalist and not a socialist revolution. Given this collection of strains it was a surprise the movement lasted as long as it did, and for this it owed its greatest debt to the confusions over British policy.

THE TREATY, 1921

The truce of July 1921 and subsequent invitation to de Valera to negotiate revealed just how far the British government had travelled since 1919. The once illegal Dáil and its outlawed leaders were now recognised as the legitimate spokesmen for Ireland. This shift owed much to the moderate leadership of Austen Chamberlain, who replaced Bonar Law as Tory leader in March 1921, and the growing anxiety, even in Unionist circles, at the policy of 'unmitigated repression' [219 *p. 247*] in Ireland. For many politicians the Irish question hung like a millstone from a bygone era and needed rapid solution, as a host of problems in both the domestic and imperial sphere bore down upon the government. On the Irish side, similar moves towards negotiation had long been advocated by moderates, particularly Griffith and de Valera, as well as from pragmatic military men like Collins who realised the parlous state of the IRA by spring 1921. However, turning military stalemate into a lasting peace that satisfied all, was beyond anyone's reach in the circumstances of 1921. The furthest the British would go in settling with the south was the grant of Dominion status. Dominionhood was a form of words created by the British to disguise what, in reality, was the grant of *de facto* independence to an ex-colony. Indeed the strongest remaining tie between colony and Britain was an oath of loyalty sworn to the British Crown. This gave the relationship symbolic power and an image of continued closeness and contact whilst the truth was of two independent nation-states. But symbolism was to be all-important in the forthcoming negotiations over the future of Ireland.

The offer of Dominionhood was relayed to de Valera during his brief visit to London in early July. This was too far for many Tories, upon whom Lloyd George relied for support and who disliked him even talking to Irish 'murderers'. On the other side, Dominion status was just about acceptable for many within Sinn Féin; after all a strain of monarchism had always flowed through the party and especially Griffith. But for die-hard republicans and much of the IRA this compromised the only possible basis for agreement, an Irish republic, as sanctified by the 1916 martyrs and to which the first and second Dáils had sworn allegiance. They conveniently forgot that this was an objective the movement had singularly failed to win after nearly two years of guerrilla war. Negotiations over the treaty, therefore, stood to divide the nationalist movement, which might explain why de Valera chose not to lead the Irish delegation to London. His presence was of more use in Ireland, accommodating the movement to the necessities of a political compromise. Of course Griffith and Collins, appointed to head the team comprising Robert Barton, Eamon Duggan, Gavan Duffy and Erskine Childers, saw it differently: as Collins said defiantly, 'let them make a scapegoat or anything they wish of me' [281 *p. 69*].

The task of the delegation was all the more bewildering given the confusion surrounding their freedom of action [*Doc. 24*]. They agreed with de Valera to refer any settlement back to the Irish government before ratification, yet this contradicted their prior endowment of *full* plenipotentiary powers by the Dáil to 'negotiate and conclude' a treaty. Since the Dáil was the 'Sovereign' body, the delegation had the right, in a strictly constitutional sense, to sign the treaty. Such confusions were not helped by divisions amongst the delegates. Collins and Griffith shared a deep mistrust of Childers, the result of their suspicions that he was de Valera's stooge. Thus circumstances were far from ideal when the delegation finally met Lloyd George, Chamberlain, Churchill and Lord Birkenhead on 11 October, the first of a series of meetings up until 6 December.

Negotiations centred upon two issues: partition and the constitutional status of Ireland as regards the United Kingdom. Though Griffith and Collins, by this stage, were probably willing to accept Dominion status, it had been rejected by the Dáil and Irish Cabinet back in July. In its place de Valera had offered a much looser arrangement of 'external association'. Here the British Crown would have no internal role over an independent Ireland and the Irish Assembly would not swear an oath of loyalty to it, though they would recognise the Crown as head of an association known as the British Commonwealth of Nations. The British government could not accept this in the environment of 1921, particularly the rejection of an oath. But in order to 'move' the delegation on this issue, Lloyd George tried to hatch a deal. He raised the question of Irish unity, hoping to use it as an incentive, first trying to induce Craig to join an all-Irish settlement but, unsurprisingly, achieving little success. As an alternative Lloyd George offered to the Irish delegates a Boundary Commission that would investigate the lines of partition. This, Lloyd George assured

Griffith and Collins, would lead to the 'essential unity' of Ireland, by reducing the northern state to an unworkable four counties which, having collapsed, would move naturally under Dublin's authority. Secondly, Lloyd George suggested the Irish Assembly could make a revised oath of loyalty to the Crown as a precondition to their acceptance of Dominion status. This revised oath required Irish representatives to be '*faithful* to H.M. King George V, his heirs and successors by law, in virtue of the common citizenship of Ireland with Great Britain and her adherence to and *membership of* the group of nations forming the British Commonwealth of nations'. In other words fidelity rather than allegiance to the King, in exchange for Dominion status. Together with a Boundary Commission this represented the furthest limit Lloyd George would, and indeed could, go.

After several weeks of intense conference, Lloyd George sensed the pressure and exhaustion that Griffith and Collins were under. He now pressed home his offer in the form of an ultimatum. The choice lay, he declared on the evening of 5 December, between signing the treaty that very night or the resumption of war between their two countries. In typically dramatic fashion he produced two letters enshrining both alternatives, for immediate delivery to Craig. This helped bring Collins into line, realising this was the best they would get from the British and only too aware of the difficulty renewed hostilities would pose to an exhausted IRA. His decision, reached in the taxi *en route* to their lodgings, was enough to bring over Duggan, Barton and Duffy; Childers as secretary had no vote. Returning that same evening to Downing Street, at 2.20 a.m. on Tuesday 6 December, the Irish delegation, after tortuous argument and soul-searching, signed the Anglo-Irish Treaty [*Doc. 25*].

The Act of Union was repealed. In its place the 26 counties became the Irish Free State, a Dominion member of the British Commonwealth. It was composed of a lower house of 153 members, elected on proportional representation, an upper house of 60 senators, partly elected by the Dáil and partly nominated by the President of the Executive, the Irish equivalent to the British Prime Minister and Cabinet. They were given almost complete autonomy over domestic matters, powers far in excess of anything contemplated by O'Connell or Parnell. Britain maintained a representative as Governor-General, a position which went to Tim Healy, as well as three naval bases at Queenstown, Berehaven and Lough Swilly.

To both countries it [the Treaty] spelt overwhelming immediate benefits. To England relief immeasurable from an unending political distraction and an age-long sense of shame. Never again would more British ministries fall on Irish than on English issues. Never again would Englishmen feel that there was one subject to be passed over in talking to their truest friends abroad. Ireland had graduated from a plague-spot to a polity ... To Ireland it brought common sense, physical emancipation – its lighter burdens, its solid fruits. Dublin Castle would yield up her grim accumulated secrets. The hand of the British legislator, British administrator and British judge would lie no more heavy on Ireland; the British military and British police would patrol her paths no more. Lloyd George could salute an Ireland 'free within her boundaries to marshal her own resources, direct her own forces and guide her own destinies'. And Griffith could, with equal justice claim ... they had brought back the flag; they brought back Ireland a status of equality with England; they had secured the evacuation of Ireland after seven hundred years. [241 *p. 247*]

We might question the optimism of Pakenham's account. For the British, the Treaty facilitated the end of the coalition government in October 1922 and sank Lloyd George's career, distrusted by Labour and Liberals for his excessive policies and by Tories for not finishing the job. It also left the problem of Northern Ireland, a devolved polity within the UK with a large proportion of its population loyal, in political, religious and cultural terms, to the Irish Free State. This problem, though dormant for the next 50 years, would explode into life by the late 1960s with the Troubles. More immediately dramatic, the Treaty raised intense debate in Ireland about whether to accept Dominion status or hold out for a republic, and this split the republican movement into anti- and pro-Treaty sections and plunged Ireland into full-scale civil war by June 1922 [228]. However, there is no disputing the central message of the Treaty: the Act of Union between Britain and Ireland ended on 6 December 1921.

PART THREE: ASSESSMENT

It was once thought by historians that 'national deliverance' was part of the natural process of world development. Different nationalities and 'peoples' would *inevitably* establish a government of their own, as occurred throughout much of central and eastern Europe after 1919 and across the rest of the world after 1945; the only point of contention was the timing of such a development. By this understanding, Ireland was one of the first 'nations' to win its freedom within the British Empire, having struck the initial blow in 1916 and then driven the imperial power from its shores by 1921. As such she became an inspiration to other nationalist movements within the Empire, as with the Indian National Congress or the Haganah in Palestine. Irish success in winning Dominion Home Rule in 1921 was subsequently back-projected by historians onto events of the nineteenth century, weaving the story of Ireland since the Act of Union into one long tale of Irish resistance to English domination. In this way, all roads led, inevitably, to the Treaty, with O'Connell's struggle for repeal of the Union connected to Parnell's efforts to win Home Rule and to the rebels of Easter 1916, and even beyond to the new Irish Constitution of 1937 and the Republic of Ireland Act of 1949, both of which 'mopped-up' from where the Treaty had left off.

But to accept this understanding as *the* central meaning of the Anglo-Irish connection is to accept a rather narrow interpretive account of Ireland's past, while denying the essential contingency and ambivalence of the historial process and the broad variety of experiences and complexity in the Anglo-Irish relationship. Such an approach, for example, condemns the British project in Ireland to one foredoomed to inevitable failure, so ignoring those moments when the project appeared to be working or the missed opportunities when Anglo-Irish politics might very well have taken a radically different course. The Whig–Nationalist alliance of the 1830s, the 'Union of Hearts' between Gladstone and Parnell, the cooperation between

William O'Brien and Lord Dunraven, and Redmond's close commitment to Liberal politics from 1910, all seemed to herald a new direction. More fundamentally, the introduction of Catholic emancipation in 1801 or Home Rule in 1886 might well have stabilised the Union and fully integrated Ireland into the United Kingdom.

Reintroducing variety and a certain 'messiness' into our understanding of nineteenth-century and early-twentieth-century Anglo-Irish politics has allowed fresh perspectives to be opened up. This is particularly true with Irish nationalism, which no longer appears the all-encompassing and relentless force it was once thought to be. Research has shown that on many occasions nationalist organisations were divided and weak, with little to indicate future triumph. For example, the period following O'Connell's fall at Clontarf in 1843, the sterility (in nationalist terms) of the 1850s and 1860s, the deep splits in the Nationalist party during the 1890s and the divisions of the era from 1914 provide few signs of inexorable victory. Nor was nationalism the sole motivation of Irish people, for it shared the Irish ideological stage with other beliefs. Liberalism was a powerful force in the 1820s and 1830s; indeed O'Connell's career fits as easily into a liberal garb as it does a nationalist one. Butt and Parnell were as much conservatives as they were nationalists. Connolly's vision of the nation was reached through a revolutionary socialist perspective. More generally, republicanism and Catholicism deeply infused national sentiment: arguably, for some, a commitment to a republic took precedence over their commitment to a nation-state. And perhaps even more important than nationalism in Irish politics were questions of wage levels, land values and ownership, family and village rivalries, grazing rights, food prices and religious controversies. These were the everyday issues that concerned ordinary Irishmen and women. Only at certain moments did nationalist sentiments break through this web of 'immediacy' to influence and sway popular attitudes, as in the 1820s, again from 1879 when Ireland fell under the spell of Parnell, and in the period after spring 1918. In other words, it took rather unique circumstances and even more unique individuals before 'the politics of the next field became synonymous with the politics of the independent land of Ireland' [168 *p. 153*].

Of course, to suggest fresh perspectives and to question the 'established truths' of the traditional nationalist canon should not be read as pro-British. For Ulster Unionism, a body of opinion similarly concerned with constructing its own sympathetic past, has also come in for sustained re-interpretation, revealing a movement much more divided and vulnerable to internal fissure [20; 124; 163; 173]. Moreover, the central aim of historical research over the last two decades has not been to exonerate or excuse but to *explain* events in Ireland. And no amount of creative historical speculation could suggest that British policy, whatever the criteria, was anything but a failure. Despite moments of promise and a fair degree of good intention, successive British governments revealed an enduring inclination to do the wrong thing in Ireland. This can be seen with the failure to accompany the Act of Union with the emancipation of Catholics, or the failure to approach the immense problems of the Great Famine with sufficient sensitivity and political judgement, or a failure to satisfy tenant land grievances or appease the Catholic Church or grant Home Rule.

On many occasions muddle and ineptitude lay at the heart of British policy, be it the Universities Bill of 1873, the controversy surrounding the Compensation for Disturbance Bill of 1880, the procedural mistakes with the Irish Local Government Act of 1898 or, from 1918, the division of power and responsibility in Ireland between political, military and policing services. At other times policy failed due to a lack of political judgement or foresight. This might include Gladstone's imprisonment of Parnell, which gave the nationalist leader's declining influence a much-needed boost; Arthur Balfour's failure to build on the consensual political atmosphere established by Lord Dunraven, William O'Brien and George Wyndham; Asquith's failure to introduce the exclusion of Ulster at the start of his third Home Rule Bill, so preventing the development of the UVF; and the decision in 1916 to pass political control to the military authorities, one of their first acts being to execute fifteen of the rebels against a backdrop of increasingly sympathetic public sentiment. But the most damaging miscalculation was the decision taken by Lloyd George to impose conscription onto Ireland in the spring of 1918.

Aware of such blunders, apologists of British policy place the blame on such unhistorical and insulting claims as a 'natural' tendency to disloyalty or duplicity in the Irish character. One famous adage holds that 'every time the English came within sight of solving the Irish question, the Irish changed the question'. But this simply testifies to the slowness, lack of foresight and general conservatism of British administrators to legislate properly for Ireland, rather than any deception on the part of the Irish people.

The answer as to why British policy failed in Ireland surely lies with the difficulties of the enterprise. The assimilation of Ireland into the UK was a far more challenging exercise than the assimilation of either Wales or Scotland. This was not immediately obvious, for Wales and Scotland had also enjoyed linguistic differences with

England as well as a distinct sense of a common cultural experience and 'past'. However, and most fundamentally, both of these principalities were, despite various denominational differences, of the Protestant faith, whereas Ireland was three-quarters Catholic. This made the Welsh and Scots willing collaborators in the series of religious wars with Spain and France from the late seventeenth century, and defining themselves as defenders of British Protestantism 'struggling against the world's foremost Catholic powers', but, as a consequence, stigmatising much of Ireland as a Catholic, 'foreign-leaning' Other. Thus, whereas this evolving sense of Britishness acted as an integrative identity for England, Scotland and Wales, for Ireland it served to exclude [64]. Wales and Scotland also participated in Britain's economic expansion and modernisation, whereas Ireland remained firmly outside that process, apart from the area around Belfast. Not only, then, did southern and western Ireland differ on religious grounds from Wales, England and Scotland but those differences were underscored and reinforced by growing economic disparities: even those parts of Scotland and Wales that also stood outside modernisation, at least possessed a common Protestantism.

Lastly, unlike Wales and Scotland, Ireland could exert a great deal of political influence. Irish MPs, at certain moments, held enough strength of numbers and unity of purpose to exert a degree of leverage in Parliament, as with O'Connell in the 1820s and 1830s, the independent Irish party of the 1850s and the Home Government party of Butt. After the 1884/85 Franchise and Redistribution Acts, this influence grew as elections now regularly supplied the Irish Nationalist party with over 80 seats, a number sufficient to pressure a Liberal government into adopting Home Rule on three occasions. As significant were Irish Unionists, who maintained a political influence at Westminster far in excess of their numerical position. The House of Lords showed a heavy bias in their favour, notably in blocking the second Home Rule Bill. And the Conservative party was often a willing collaborator in upholding the Union with Ireland: the period 1912–22 saw Ulster Unionist sway over the Tory leadership at its most effective and influential. In light of this we might speculate that, rather ironically, it was Irish political *strength* that prevented the successful assimilation of Ireland into the UK or at the very least impeded a peaceful, timely and satisfactory solution to the Irish question. The political influence of Irish Nationalists meant British politics could never ignore Irish national claims, while the influence of Irish Unionism prevented any initiative to satisfy those claims being carried forward or to reform the existing relationship between Britain and Ireland.

Caught between a rock and a hard place, it is perhaps no surprise that British policy in Ireland was characterised by muddle and mis-judgement or that it vacillated, sometimes dramatically, between over-reaction and reformism, between coercion and concession. The need to satisfy or simply appease these two seemingly intractible sides prompted such vacillation. Yet given these obstacles to a successful absorption of Ireland into the UK, what is surprising was Britain's decision to persevere with the Union with Ireland for so long and at such a cost, in terms of men, money, international reputation and political energy.

No straightforward or obvious answer is possible to explain this commitment. Defence of religious rights and freedoms was one moti-vation. But this did not prevent disestablishment of the Irish Church in 1869 or the desertion of northern Catholics in 1920 and southern Protestants in 1921, both to reside under regimes that restricted relig-ious liberty. Defence of property and wealth was often mooted as a reason for the British presence in Ireland. Yet Gladstone had shown a willingness to extend the powers of the State with slight regard to the private ownership of land, while Tory governments under Salisbury and Balfour facilitated the transfer of land from the existing landown-ers to a new class of tenant proprietor. It was also thought, especially by Tories, that repealing the Act of Union would lead to the fragmen-tation of the British Empire. However, this is to ignore the successful transfer of power to Canada, Australia, New Zealand and South Africa, without endangering the Empire. National security was per-haps a more central motivation, and in a period when France was the main national enemy, at least up until the late 1890s, Catholic Ireland represented an obvious strategic danger to the British mainland. But Nationalists like Parnell and Redmond argued that Home Rule would actually strengthen the bonds of loyalty between Ireland and Britain. Trust would foster far closer relations than political domination ever could, and the action of the Dominions coming to Britain's aid in 1914 lends a certain veracity to such a view. The most likely explanation of Britain's determination to hold on to Ireland would be a mixture of these motives, acting in different strengths in different circumstances.

PART FOUR: DOCUMENTS

DOCUMENT 1   A NATIONALIST INTERPRETATION

The extract comes from an article written by Brendan Bradshaw in 1989. It was intended as an attack on the 'revisionist' orthodoxy which Bradshaw believed had stultified research into Ireland's past. In place of an empirical, value-free approach, he called for empathy and imagination from historians in understanding and explaining Irish history, one that did not dilute the trauma or hide behind a claim to objectivity a pro-British stance. Note that he talks of revisionists as engaged in an 'enterprise' within an organised school, suggesting such practitioners hold a narrow intent to undermine nationalist views.

The contention of this study is that the aspiration towards the development of a value free history has followed the achievement of the professional school of Irish historians since its establishment in the early 1930s. That principle has shown itself to be inappropriate as a means of appraising the Irish historical experience in two major respects. On the one hand, the inherent limitations of the principle have been revealed in the inhibitions displayed by its practitioners in face of the catastrophic dimension of Irish history. On the other hand, its vulnerability to tacit bias has been highlighted by the negative revisionism practised in its name in explaining the Irish national tradition. Perhaps the most disturbing aspect of the entire enterprise is the credibility gap which is now acknowledged by all sides to exist between the new professional history and the general public. All of these considerations lead to the conclusion which has been implicit in the discussion from the outset. The value free principle must be abandoned as a basis on which to develop a professional historiography in Ireland. ... As the fruits have already shown, an imaginative and empathetic approach holds out the prospect of a professional historiography which concedes nothing in the way of critical standards of scholarship, while at the same time responding sensitively to the totality of the Irish historical experience. The time has come, therefore, to resume contact with an emerging tradition of Irish historical scholarship which was thrust aside by the impatient young men of the 1930s, and to recover the vision of its two great luminaries, Eoin MacNeill and Edmund Curtis. ... It is not a plea for Green history

... The plea, therefore, is for an account of Irish history capable of comprehending sympathetically the historical experience of both communities, and, by comprehending them, of mediating between the island's past and its present.

Brendan Bradshaw, 'Nationalism and Historical Scholarship in Modern Ireland', *Irish Historical Studies*, Vol XXVI, 104, 1989, pp. 350–1.

DOCUMENT 2 'REVISIONIST' COUNTER-BLAST

Roy Foster is widely acknowledged as one of the leading lights of the 'revisionist' school, though he himself rejects the notion of revisionism and of a distinct 'school' of historians. His most famous attack on the traditional nationalist interpretation of Ireland's past came in 1988 with his Modern Ireland, 1600–1972. *The extract is taken from a collection of essays published in 1993 and discusses the developments of a 'nationalist history' as well as some of the central concerns of so-called revisionists.*

What followed was the institutionalisation of a certain view of history in the Free State, as instructed by the Department of Education from 1922, and memorialised in textbooks that did duty for the next forty years. Teachers were informed that 'the continuity of the separatist idea from Tone to Pearse should be stressed'; pupils should be 'imbued with the ideals and aspirations of such men as Thomas Davis and Patrick Pearse'. Thus history was debased into a two-dimensional, linear development, and the function of its teaching interpreted as 'undoing the conquest'; even the architecture of the Irish eighteenth century was stigmatised as ideologically degenerate. ... the popularisation of invented tradition in the Free State and the Republic served a directly political function important enough to bear analysis; and it came about as the result of a longer process than is sometimes assumed. ...

By the 1960s the work of a whole generation of scholars had exploded the basis for popular assumptions about early Irish society, the conquest, the plantations, the eighteenth-century parliament, the record of landlordism, and most of all the continuities between the various manifestations of nationalism: in some cases, reverting to ideas held in the past by minority opinion but contemptuously dismissed. ... What happened, at least until very recently, seemed a contrary process: academic revisionism has coincided with popular revivalism. The version of Irish history presented in P.S. O'Hegarty's influential *Ireland under the Union* persisted: 'the story of a people coming out of captivity, out of the underground, finding every artery of national life occupied by the enemy, recovering them one by one, and coming out at last into the full blaze of the sun ...' This version long remained in vogue among politicians and popular historians (and *a fortiori* television historians). The simplified notions have their own resilience: they are buried deep in the core of popular consciousness, as recent analysis of folk attitudes in rural Ireland has shown. The point should also be made that the triumph of revisionism in Irish academic historiography is a particularly exact instance of the owl of Minerva flying only in the shades of nightfall: events in the island since 1969 have both emphasised the power of ideas of history, and the time it takes for scholarly revolutions to affect everyday attitudes. Nor have Irish readers always been particularly anxious to explore the historical analysis offered by scholars from other countries. But the discrepancy between beliefs in the university and outside it raises some questions. The transition from piety to iconoclasm may have been too abrupt for the change to percolate through immediately. Still the depressing lesson is probably that history as conceived by scholars is different to what it is understood to be at large, where 'myth' is probably the correct, if over-used anthropological term.

R.F. Foster, 'History and the Irish Question', in *Paddy and Mr Punch: Connections in Irish and English History* (Penguin, London, 1993), pp. 1–20.

DOCUMENT 3   FENIAN PROCLAMATION OF AN IRISH REPUBLIC

As Fenians prepared for a Rising in 1867, two of their leaders, Thomas Kelly and Gustave Cluseret, composed a Proclamation of an Irish Republic for release across Britain. It differed from the later republican Proclamation made by Pearse in that it pitched its message towards the British working class, who it hoped would take up arms alongside the Fenians. These sentiments would find an echo 50 years later in the writings of James Connolly.

I.R – Proclamation! The Irish People to the World.

We have suffered centuries of outrage, enforced poverty, and bitter misery. Our rights and liberties have been trampled on by an alien aristocracy, who, treating us as foes, usurped our lands, and drew away from our unfortunate country all material riches. The real owners of the soil were removed to make room for cattle, and driven across the ocean to seek the means of living and the political rights denied them at home; while our men of thought and action were condemned to loss of life and liberty. But we never lost the memory and hope of a national existence. We appealed in vain to the reason and sense of justice of the dominant powers. Our mildest remonstrances were met with sneers and contempt. Our appeals to arms were always unsuccessful. Today, having no honourable alternative left, we again appeal to force as our last resource. We accept the conditions of appeal, manfully deeming it better to die in the struggle for freedom than to continue an existence of utter serfdom. All men are born with equal rights, and in associating together to protect one another and share public burdens, justice demands that such associations should rest upon a basis which maintains equality instead of destroying it. We therefore declare that, unable longer to endure the curse of monarchical government, we aim at founding a republic, based on universal suffrage, which shall secure to all the intrinsic value of their labour. The soil of Ireland, at present in the possession of an oligarchy, belongs to us, the Irish people, and to us it must be restored. We declare also in favour of absolute liberty of conscience, and the complete separation of Church and State. We appeal to the Highest Tribunal for evidence of the justice of our cause. History bears testimony to the intensity of our sufferings, and we declare in the face of our brethren, that we intend no war against the people of England; our war is against the aristocratic locusts, whether English or Irish, who have eaten the verdure of our fields – against the aristocratic leeches who drain alike our blood and theirs. Republicans of the entire world, our cause is your cause. Our enemy is your enemy. Let your hearts be with us. As for you, workmen of England, it is not only your hearts we wish, but your arms. Remember the starvation and degradation brought to your firesides by the oppression of labour. Remember the past, look well to the future, and avenge yourselves by giving liberty to your children in the coming struggle for human freedom.

Herewith we proclaim the Irish Republic.

J. Newsinger, *Fenianism in Mid-Victorian Britain* (Pluto, London, 1994), pp. 54–5.

DOCUMENT 4   **PARNELL AT ENNIS**

Parnell's speech at Ennis on 19 September 1880 was arguably one of the most famous of all his career. It fully committed him to the land agitation and called on the Irish tenant class to impose a policy of 'social ostracism' upon the landlords. Anyone who broke this 'code' was to be placed into 'moral Coventry'.

'Depend upon it that the measure of the land bill of next session will be the measure of your activity and energy this winter (cheers) – it will be the measure of your determination not to pay unjust rents – it will be the measure of your determination to keep a firm grip on your homesteads (cheers). It will be the measure of your determination not to bid for farms from which others have been evicted, and to use the strong force of public opinion to deter any unjust men amongst yourselves – and there are many such – from bidding for such farms (hear, hear). If you refuse to pay unjust rents, if you refuse to take farms from which others have been evicted, the land question must be settled, and settled in a way that will be satisfactory to you. It depends, therefore, upon yourselves, and not upon any commission or any government. When you have made this question ripe for settlement then and not till then will it be settled (cheers). It is very nearly ripe already in many parts of Ireland. It is ripe in Mayo, Galway, Roscommon, Sligo, and portions of the county Cork (cheers). But I regret to say that the tenant farmers of the county Clare have been backward in organisation up to the present time. You must take and band yourselves together in Land Leagues. Every town and village must have its own branch. You must know the circumstances of the holdings and of the tenures of the district over which the League has jurisdiction – you must see that the principles of the Land League are inculcated, and when you have done this in Clare, then Clare will take higher rank with the other active counties, and you will be included in the next land bill brought forward by the government (cheers). Now, what are you to do to a tenant who bids for a farm from which another tenant has been evicted?'

Several voices. 'Shoot him.'

Mr. Parnell: 'I think I heard somebody say shoot him (cheers). I wish to point out to you a very much better way – a more Christian and charitable way, which will give the lost man an opportunity of repenting (laughter, and hear). When a man takes a farm from which another has been evicted you must shun him on the roadside when you meet him – you must shun him in the streets of the town – you must shun him in the shop – you must shun him in the fairgreen and in the market place and even in the place of worship, by leaving him alone, by putting him into a moral Coventry, by isolating him from the rest of his country as if he were the leper of old – you must show him your detestation of the crime he has committed.'

Freeman's Journal, 20 September 1880.

DOCUMENT 5   HOME RULE AND LIBERAL UNIONISM

The extract is taken from the diary of the fifteenth Earl of Derby, the ex-Tory Foreign Secretary under Disraeli and then, from 1882, Colonial Secretary under Gladstone. The selections explore the fears many Whigs had for Home Rule and their organisation against it. It is particularly useful as an insight into the views of Lord Hartington, whom Derby would follow out of the Liberal party from June 1886.

18 December 1885 (Friday) ... In the papers, yesterday's news, ascribing to Gladstone a plan of Home Rule as being prepared and ready for production, with some details as to its nature. It is contradicted on authority but in such a manner scarcely to amount to a denial of the fact. It is however so far satisfactory that it negatives the idea of any such plan being sprung upon us as a surprise.

Wrote to Hartington, stating my strong objections to an Irish parliament, my conviction that it would not long remain subject to any limitations that might be imposed upon its power, and that its establishment would only serve as the basis for a fresh agitation. I invited his opinion, and asked him as to Spencer's, saying that much depended on him at this juncture, that I, being in the Lords, could take refuge in silence: he could not: if he thought this concession inevitable, I did not see that resistance was possible, and should probably drop out of the affair altogether. But if he was ready to express himself against it, I should support him. This was the substance of my letter, which was long, and of which I kept no copy. We shall see what he answers. Of his personal opinion I have no doubt, but he has been dragged so far by his colleagues, and by the natural dislike which he must feel to give up his position in the party, that I feel no confidence in his power of resistance.

22 December 1885 ... Hartington's letter, which I answered today, is much longer than Granville's, and more explicit. He does not know, he says, exactly what Gladstone has been doing, but his action 'has put us all in a position of the greatest difficulty'. He does not think that G. has a definite scheme, but that he has been discussing the whole question very freely in conversation and correspondence. He agrees with me 'that the plan of a subordinate legislature in Dublin is inadmissible, and that an independent legislature would be preferable. The first alternative would be certain to lead to the second'. He is not disposed to give way to Parnell without a farther struggle, though 'seeing the most tremendous difficulties in the way of resistance'. He expects a worse state of disorder and outrage to follow on the refusal of Parnell's demands than has yet been known in Ireland: and doubts whether parliament will give to any government the necessary powers to deal with it. He then refers to a letter of his lately published, which he says is meant to show 'that I am not only committed but am opposed to the scheme': and to prevent the whole party drifting into acquiescence with what he fears are rightly supposed to be Gladstone's opinions. He is afraid that Spencer is likely to give way. I answered briefly, thanking and agreeing, and asking him here.

The Later Derby Diaries: Home Rule, Liberal Unionism and Aristocratic Life in Late Victorian England, ed. J. Vincent (University of Bristol, Bristol, 1981), pp. 0047–0049.

DOCUMENT 6 GLADSTONE AND HOME RULE, 1886

Having returned to government in January 1886, freshly converted to Irish Home Rule and reliant upon Parnell's support in the House of Commons, Gladstone introduced a Home Rule Bill on 8 April 1886. The speech was a passionate appeal for a new chapter in Anglo-Irish relations lasting over three and a half hours and in content was, according to Gladstone's latest biographer, 'remarkable for its expository detail and for its peroration'. Though the bill's reception left grounds for optimism, it was defeated on its second reading on 8 June by 341 to 311, with 93 Liberals, led by Lord Hartington and Joseph Chamberlain, voting against their own government.

We are sensible that we have taken an important decision – our choice has been made. It has not been made without thought; it has been made in the full knowledge that trial and difficulty may confront us on our path. We have no right to say that Ireland, through her constitutionally-chosen representative, will accept the plan I offer. Whether it will be so I do not know – I have no title to assume it, but if Ireland does not cheerfully accept it, it is impossible for us to attempt to force on her what she does not heartily welcome and embrace. There are difficulties; but I rely upon the patriotism and sagacity of this House; I rely on the effects of full and free discussion; and I rely more than all upon the just and generous sentiments of the two British nations. Looking forward, I ask the House to assist us in the work which we have undertaken, and to believe that no trivial motive can have driven us to it – to assist us in this work which, we believe, will restore parliament to its dignity and legislation to its free and unimpeded course. I ask you to show to Europe and to America that we, too, can face political problems which America twenty years ago faced and which many countries in Europe have been called upon to face, and have not feared to deal with. I ask that in our own case we should practise, with firm and fearless hand, what we have so often preached – the doctrine which we have so often inculcated upon others – namely, that the concession of local self-government is not the way to sap or impair, but the way to strengthen and consolidate unity. I ask that happy experience which we have gained in England and in Scotland, where the course of generations has now taught us, not as a dream of a theory, but as a practice and as life, that the best and surest foundation we can find to build upon is the foundation afforded by the affections, the convictions, and the will of the nation; and it is thus, by the decree of the Almighty, that we may be enabled to secure at once the social peace, the fame, the power, and the permanence of the empire.

Parliamentary Debates, 3rd Series, CCCIV, cols 1037ff., 8 April 1886.

DOCUMENT 7   ARGUMENTS AGAINST HOME RULE

The following extracts are taken from a pamphlet published in 1886 by the Irish Loyal and Patriotic Union, entitled Union or Separation. *It offered a broad attack of Home Rule and the Nationalist party, but gives particular attention to the apparent 'lower-class' nature of the Home Rule agitation and the danger it posed to Unionist wealth and land.*

Between those Roman Catholic laymen who have the courage to avow their sentiments of loyalty, and the fanatical rabble who rave against England – it is no longer against the 'Saxon' – there is a large mass of opinion, much of which is in favour of the Union, and much, no doubt, hostile to it; but, owing to the terrorism that prevails, it is impossible to say with certainty what proportion is on either side. Of one thing, however, we may be absolutely certain, that all the Roman Catholics of wealth and position, all the men of intelligence and culture, all who give strength and dignity to a cause, are on the side of loyalty and order. Of this we fortunately have evidence that cannot be controverted; we have but to summon Mr. Parnell's Parliamentary phalanx into court, and our case is proved. If the educated intellect, if the business energy, if the wealth of Catholic Ireland are on the side of revolution, why are they not to be found among the members sent to represent that cause in Parliament? No one knows better than Mr. Parnell how important it would be for his cause that he should be able to point to such men among his Parliamentary followers. No one will believe that he would not have been eager to secure their services if he could have done so. Why are they not there? We mention no names; but we challenge Mr. Parnell to show us among his eighty-five followers five such men. We go further: we challenge him to produce from among the whole number one man who is recognised in Ireland as a leader of Catholic opinion in any shape or form. There are plenty of such men in Ireland – men known and trusted by their co-religionists; men who have won for Irish Catholics many of the rights and privileges they possess, and who have never wavered in support of their cause. Why are these men not to be found among the representatives of Ireland in the new Parliament? The answer is, because they are unanimously opposed to the revolutionary designs of Mr. Parnell and his followers; because they are loyal to the English connection, from which they and their Church have derived so many benefits; because they foresee the condition of chaos and ruin to which their unhappy country would be reduced if it were handed over to be governed by Mr. Parnell and his communistic crew. With what audacity can Mr. Parnell and his advocates in the Press assert that he represents the opinions or the aspiration of the Catholics of Ireland, if he cannot produce from among his eighty-five followers one single representative Catholic – one man recognised as a leader or exponent of Catholic opinion, or authorised to speak on behalf of the Catholics of Ireland?...

Those politicians in England who think that they are bound to entertain Mr. Parnell's demands, because he makes them in the name of the 'Irish people' should ponder well on these facts. If Mr. Parnell does not speak with the authority of the Protestants of Ireland, who form one-fourth of the population; if he does not speak in the name of the respectable and intelligent Catholics of Ireland, who certainly form at least another fourth of the population, in whose name and by what authority does he speak?...

Let us grant for a moment, what we by no means admit, that Mr. Parnell represents the sentiments of the remaining half of the people of Ireland – let us see of what that half is composed. We say with perfect knowledge that it consists of the lowest half of the population; of tenant-farmers on a small scale, who aim at acquiring the ownership of the land they till without the usual preliminary operation of paying for it; of labourers who covet the land occupied by the farmers, and who see no adequate reason why they should not get their share of the plunder; but chiefly of the disaffected masses who have been taught for the past forty years by the seditious newspapers that find their way into every Irish peasant's house, to hate everything English, and to believe that separation from England would restore an era of national greatness and prosperity, such as is popularly believed to have existed in Ireland sometime before the birth of Christ ...

Let there be no mistake in this matter. An Irish Parliament will be composed of the same elements as are found among the Irish Members now gathered under the banner unfurled by Mr. Parnell: only its members will be more numerous, more hostile to the friends of England, more unscrupulous if that be possible – and more rapacious, less restrained by decency or prudence than they are now. And there is this further consideration, that then they will have full power to give effect to their hostility. If some eighty or ninety of the six hundred and seventy Members of the United Parliament can set the authority of the rest at defiance, how will they be controlled in an assembly of their own, where they will be in a majority of four to one?

P. Buckland, *Irish Unionism, 1885–1923: A Documentary History* (H.M. Stationery Office, Belfast, 1973), p. 20.

DOCUMENT 8   SOCIALISM AND NATIONALISM

Having arrived in Ireland from Scotland, James Connolly quickly emerged as a leading light in the Irish Labour movement. As a revolutionary socialist he founded the Irish Socialist Republican party in 1896, and took a prominent part in the Dublin strikes of 1908 and the lock-out of 1913. Throughout his career Connolly saw an essential link between nationalism and socialism: to achieve socialism, Ireland would first have to break the strong imperialist hold of Britain. Such an understanding of Ireland's path to freedom encouraged Connolly, by 1916, to throw in his lot with Pearse and to join his Irish Citizen Army, formed to protect workers during the Dublin lock-out, with the Volunteers.

An Irish Republic, the only purely political change in Ireland worth crossing the street for, will never be realised except by a revolutionary party that proceeds upon the promise that the capitalist and the landlord classes in town and country in Ireland are *particeps criminis* (criminal accomplices) with the British government, in the enslavement and the subjection of the nation. Such a revolutionary party must be Socialist, and from Socialism alone can the salvation of Ireland come.

The struggle for Irish freedom has two aspects: it is national and it is social. The national idea can never be realised until Ireland stands forth before the world as a nation, free and independent. It is social and economic, because no matter what form the government may be, as long as one class owns as private property the land and instruments of labour from which mankind derive their substance, that class will always have it in their power to plunder and enslave the kinder of their fellow creatures.

Both extracts come from the socialist pamphlet *The Harp*, and are printed in W.K. Anderson, *James Connolly and the Irish Left* (Irish Academic Press, Dublin, 1994), pp. 41–2.

DOCUMENT 9   GAELICISING IRELAND

The work of the Gaelic League, with its intention of 'de-Anglicanising Ireland', was carried forward by a host of Gaelic enthusiasts, journalists and publicists, of whom Patrick Pearse was perhaps the most famous example. In 1903, after several years of tireless energy on behalf of the League, he took control of the Gaelic publication An Claidheamh Soluis. The extract, calling for the preservation of the Gaelic language and support for the League, is taken from one of his first articles in the journal.

When the position of Ireland's language as her greatest heritage is once fixed, all other matters will insensibly adjust themselves. As it develops, and *because* it develops, it will carry all kindred movements with it. Irish music, Irish art, Irish dancing, Irish games and customs, Irish industries, Irish politics – all these are worthy objects. Not one of them, however, can be said to be fundamental.

When Ireland's language is established her own distinctive culture is assured. ... All phases of a nation's life will most assuredly adjust themselves on national lines as best suited to the national character as safeguarded by its strongest bulwark. ...

To preserve and spread the language, then, is the single idea of the Gaelic League. While other causes are borne along by it as the water-fowl is carried by the current, it alone is our inspiration. ... We have a task before us that requires self-sacrifice and exertion as heroic as any nation ever put forth. ... Woe to the unfortunate Irishman who by his lethargy, his pride, his obstinacy, or his selfish prejudice, allows the moments to pass, or impedes this national work until it is too late.

Ruth Dudley Edwards, *Patrick Pearse: The Triumph of Failure* (Faber & Faber, London, 1977), p. 70.

DOCUMENT 10   MOVEMENT BACK TO TRADITIONALISM

Dillon's speech at Swinford, County Mayo, in August 1903 marked an attack by the more traditional forces within the Nationalist party against O'Brien's moves to find a more consensual approach to Irish politics. It marked a lost opportunity when a new type of politics might have emerged in Ireland. The revival of traditionalism was reflected in Ulster with vicious attacks upon George Wyndham and his permanent secretary Sir Anthony MacDonnell, and the formation of the UUC by 1905.

We hear a great deal about conciliation. To the amazement of some of us old campaigners, we hear Irish landlords talking of conciliation, and of intention to go into conferences with the leaders of the Irish Party. That is the new feature, and some men are asked to believe it is due to what the Methodists describe as a new birth an infusion of grace into the landlord party. I don't believe a word of it, I believe the origin and source of it was the fact that the landlords of Ireland were behind the scenes, and they knew that the whole policy of coercion was going to topple down about their ears ... When the landlords talk of conciliation, what do they want? They want 25 years purchase of the land. ... for my part ... I am so far sceptical that I have no faith in the doctrine of conciliation.

F.S.L. Lyons, *John Dillon: A Biography* (Routledge, Dublin, 1968), p. 236.

DOCUMENT 11   CARSON AND THE ULSTER REVOLT

Sir Edward Carson, leader of the Irish Unionists from February 1910, led an extreme and bitter campaign of resistance against the third Home Rule Bill. The extract is taken from one of his many speeches during this period delivered at a huge meeting at Craigavon on 23 September 1911. Note his reference to the creation of a Provisional Government but only of those districts they controlled, which meant six or even just four counties in Ulster. Though a southern Unionist, he was clearly thinking of a future partition of Ireland, as early as 1911.

Mr. Asquith, the Prime Minister, says that we are not to be allowed to put our case before the British electorate. Very well. By that determination he drives you in the ultimate result to rely upon your own strength, and we must follow all that out to its logical conclusion. ... That involves something more than that we do not accept Home Rule.

We must be prepared, in the event of a Home Rule Bill passing, with such measure as will carry on for ourselves the government of those districts of which we have control. We must be prepared – and time is precious in these things – the morning Home Rule passes, ourselves to become responsible for the government of the Protestant Province of Ulster.

We ask your leave at the meeting of the Ulster Unionist Council, to be held on Monday, there to discuss the matter, and to set to work, to take care, so that at no time and at no intervening space shall we lack a Government in Ulster, which shall be a Government either by the Imperial Parliament or by ourselves.

H.M. Hyde, *Carson* (Heineman, London, 1953), p. 291.

DOCUMENT 12   ULSTER'S SOLEMN LEAGUE AND COVENANT

Ulster's Solemn League and Covenant, written by Sir James Craig and based on the Scottish Covenant of 1641, was signed in City Hall on 28 September

1912. It was intended as a warning to the government of Ulster's resolve and determination but given the presence of the world's press was also a propaganda spectacle to raise the profile of and support for the cause of Ulster. It would later be a source of some dispute, for southern Unionists accused the Ulstermen of betraying the Covenant when they accepted the partition of Ireland.

Being convinced in our consciences that Home Rule would be disastrous to the material well-being of Ulster as well as the whole of Ireland, subversive of our civil and religious freedom, destructive of our citizenship, and perilous to the unity of the Empire, we, whose names are underwritten, men of Ulster, loyal subjects of His Gracious Majesty, King George V, humbly relying on the God whom our fathers in days of stress and trial confidently trusted, do hereby pledge ourselves in Solemn Covenant throughout this our time of threatened calamity to stand by one another in defending for ourselves and our children our cherished position of equal citizenship in the United Kingdom, and in using all means which may be found necessary to defeat the present conspiracy to set up a Home Rule Parliament in Ireland. And in the event of such a Parliament being forced upon us we further solemnly and mutually pledge ourselves to refuse to recognise its authority. In sure confidence that God will defend the right we hereto subscribe our names. And further, we individually declare that we have not already signed this Covenant. God Save the King.

P. Buckland, *Irish Unionism, 1885–1923: A Documentary History* (H.M. Stationery Office, Belfast, 1973), p. 224.

DOCUMENT 13 **THE LARNE GUN RUNNING, APRIL 1914**

On the night of 24–25 April 1914 nearly 20,000 rifles were landed by the Ulster Volunteer Force at three locations in Ulster: Larne, Bangor and Donaghadee. The episode had been carried out under the guidance of F.H. Crawford but with the knowledge and support of Craig and Carson: it is likely that Bonar Law was also aware of some such venture. Arming the UVF strengthened the Ulstermen in their determination to resist the implementation of Home Rule over them but, more tragically, brought the gun into Irish politics.

Jack came away with Eva & me, & managed to tell me in a hurried aside, that 'they' were to 'get them in tonight'. Of course I knew what that meant, & so will you, in the light of Saturday's evening papers. His post was to be at Musgrave Channel, assisting at the Hoax which took in all the Customs Officers, & kept them occupied all night, watching the 'Balmerino' which of course contained nothing but coal!

You can imagine my anxiety, realising what was afoot, and what the dangers were, & not in the least knowing what part W. was taking in the night proceedings. I couldn't tell Eva, but she knew I was anxious, & we occupied ourselves as best we could, by catechising one another in First Aid & Home Nursing. It *was* a comfort having her. Imagine my delight when, about 6 o'clock next morning my door opened, & in came a muddy, tousled, disreputable Wolf, whose shining eyes, however told me that all was more than well. Then I learned that he had been sent to the danger-point, to Larne itself, & had been up all night, helping to unload the precious goods, & carry them to the motors waiting by the wharf. The papers will describe it all to you better than I can, & how 'they' were *all* safely landed, and *all* reached their various destinations without mishap. The whole proceedings are almost incredible, and nothing but the most perfect organisation, combined with the most perfect and loyal co-operation on the part of all concerned, could have carried it through without a single case of bloodshed. Need I say that for the organisation W. himself was mainly responsible, the scheme having been originally drawn up by him?

An extract from the diary of the wife of Capt W. Spender, April 1914, in P. Buckland, *Irish Unionism, 1885–1923: A Documentary History* (H.M. Stationery Office, Belfast, 1973), p. 257.

DOCUMENT 14   O'DONOVAN ROSSA'S FUNERAL ADDRESS

Funerals provided the IRB with a superb venue for mass demonstrations against British rule. Drawing on the example of Terence Bellew MacManus's funeral in 1861, O'Donovan Rossa's funeral in August 1915 was similarly orchestrated by Thomas MacDonagh to advertise a spirit of defiance. The address was delivered by a still relatively unknown Patrick Pearse, whose dramatic call to arms and invocation of blood sacrifice had an eerie feel, coming just eight months before the Easter Rising.

It has been thought right, before we turn away from this place in which we have laid the mortal remains of O'Donovan Rossa, that one among us should, in the name of all, speak the praise of that valiant man, and endeavour to formulate the thought and the hope that are in us as we stand around his grave. And if there is anything that makes it fitting that I rather than another, I rather than one of the grey haired men who were young with him and shared in his labour and in his suffering, should speak here, it is perhaps that I may be taken as speaking on behalf of a new generation that has been rebaptised in the Fenian faith and that has accepted the responsibility of carrying out the Fenian programme. I propose to you then that, here by the grave of this unrepentant Fenian, we renew out baptismal vows; that, here by the grave of this unconquered and unconquerable man, we ask of God, each one for himself, such unshakable purpose, such high and gallant courage, such unbreakable strength of soul as belonged to O'Donovan Rossa. Deliberately here we avow ourselves, as he avowed himself in the dock, Irishmen of one allegiance only. We of the Irish volunteers and you others who are associated with us in today's task and duty are bound together and must stand together henceforth in brotherly union for the achievement of the freedom of Ireland. And we know only one definition of freedom: it is Tone's definition, it is Mitchel's definition, it is Rossa's definition. Let no man blaspheme the cause that the dead generations of Ireland served by giving it any other name or definition than their name and their definition.

We stand at Rossa's grave not in sadness but rather in exaltation of spirit that it has been given to us to come thus into so close a communion with that brave and splendid Gael. Splendid and holy. O'Donovan Rossa was splendid in the proud manhood of him, splendid in the heroic grace of him, splendid in the Gaelic strength and clarity and truth of him. And all that splendour and pride and strength was compatible with a humility and a simplicity of devotion to Ireland, to all that was olden and beautiful and Gaelic in Ireland, the holiness and simplicity of patriotism of a Michael O'Leary or of an Eoghan O'Growney. The clear true eyes of this man almost alone in his day visioned Ireland as we of today would surely have her: not free merely, but Gaelic as well; not Gaelic merely, but free and noble as well.

In a closer spiritual communion with him now than ever before or perhaps ever again, in spiritual communion with those of his day, living and dead, who suffered with him in English prisons, in communion of spirit too with our own dear comrades who suffer in English prisons today, and speaking on their behalf as well as on our own, we pledge to Ireland our love, and we pledge to English rule in Ireland our hate. This is a place of peace, sacred to the dead, where men should speak with all charity and with all restraint but I hold it a Christian thing, as O'Donovan Rossa held it, to hate evil, to hate untruth, to hate oppression; and, hating them, to strive to overthrow them. Our foes are strong and wise and wary; but, strong and wise and wary as they are, they cannot undo the miracles of God who ripens in the hearts of young men the seeds sown by the young men of a former generation. And the seed sown by the young men of '65 and '67 are coming to their miraculous ripening today. Rulers and Defenders of Realms had need to be wary if they would guard against such processes. Life springs from death; and from the graves of patriot men and women spring living nations. The Defenders of this Realm have worked well in secret and in the open. They think that they have purchased half of us and intimidated the other half. They think that they have foreseen everything, think that they have provided against everything; but the fools, the fools, the fools! – they have left us our Fenian dead, and, while Ireland holds these graves, Ireland unfree shall never be at peace.

Pearse Museum, St Enda's, Rathfarnham, Dublin.

DOCUMENT 15   FUNERAL ADDRESS FOR THOMAS ASHE

On 25 September 1917 Thomas Ashe died after forcible feeding during his hunger strike at Mountjoy Jail. Once again Fenians organised a huge demonstration, in defiance of regulations then in operation. The address was given by Michael Collins, then emerging as the leading light in the development of the IRA. His short, blunt message speaks volumes about the type of qualities he gave to the republican movement but also nicely juxtaposes the man of action against Pearse, the man of words and dramatic gestures.

Nothing additional remains to be said. The volley which we have just heard is the only speech which it is proper to make above the grave of a dead Fenian.

F.S.L. Lyons, *Ireland Since the Famine* (Weidenfeld & Nicolson, London, 1971), p. 387.

DOCUMENT 16   PROCLAMATION OF THE REPUBLIC, 1916

On Monday 24 April 1916 sections of the Volunteers, led by Patrick Pearse, seized various buildings across Dublin, with their headquarters being the General Post Office. From its steps Pearse read out the following declaration to a small and rather bemused crowd.

Irishmen and Irishwomen: in the name of God and of the dead generations from which she receives her old tradition of nationhood, Ireland, through us, summons her children to her flag and strikes for her freedom. Having organised and trained her manhood through her secret revolutionary organisation, the Irish Republican Brotherhood, and through her open military organisations, the Irish Volunteers and Irish Citizen Army, having patiently perfected her discipline, having resolutely waited for the right moment to reveal itself, she now seizes that moment, and, supported by her exiled children in America and by gallant allies in Europe, but relying in the first on her own strength, she strikes in full confidence of victory.

We declare the right of the people of Ireland to the ownership of Ireland, and to the unfettered control of Irish destinies, to be sovereign and indefeasible. The long usurpation of that right by a foreign people and government has not extinguished the right, nor can it ever be extinguished except by the destruction of the Irish people. In every generation the Irish people have asserted their right to national freedom and sovereignty; six times during the past three hundred years they have asserted it in arms. Standing on that fundamental right and again asserting it in arms in the face of the world, we hereby proclaim the Irish Republic as a Sovereign Independent State, and we pledge our lives and the lives of our comrades-in-arms to the cause of its freedom, of its welfare, and of its exaltation among the nations.

The Irish Republic is entitled to, and hereby claims, the allegiance of every Irishman and Irishwoman. The Republic guarantees religious and civil liberty, equal rights and equal opportunities to all its citizens, and declares its resolve to pursue the happiness and prosperity of the whole nation and of all its *25* parts, cherishing all the children of the nation equally, and oblivious of the differences carefully fostered by an alien government, which have divided a minority from the majority in the past.

Until our arms have brought the opportune moment for the establishment of a permanent National Government, representative of the whole people of *30* Ireland and elected by the suffrages of all her men and women, the Provisional Government, hereby constituted, will administer the civil and military affairs of the Republic in trust for the people.

We place the cause of the Irish Republic under the protection of the Most High God, Whose blessing we invoke upon our arms, and we pray that no *35* one who serves that cause will dishonour it by cowardice, inhumanity, or rapine. In this supreme hour the Irish nation must, by its valour and discipline and by the readiness of its children to sacrifice themselves for the common good, prove itself worthy of the august destiny to which it is called.

Signed on Behalf of the Provisional Government,
Thomas J. Clarke, Sean MacDiarmada, Thomas MacDonagh, P.H. Pearse, Eamon Ceannt, James Connolly, Joseph Plunkett.

Sean Dunne (ed.), *The Ireland Anthology* (Gill & Macmillan, Dublin, 1997), pp. 264–5.

DOCUMENT 17   **SONG ON THE EASTER RISING, 1916**

The 1916 Rising quickly became a source of countless stories, ballads and folk tunes. Foggy Dew *is perhaps the most famous of these. With words written by the Rev. P. O'Neill, the song followed a long tradition whereby the exploits of Fenians and Irish nationalists were turned from military débâcle into a glorious failure, inspiring the next generation to action. The third stanza refers to Suvla, Sud-el-bar, a place and battle during the Dardanelles campaign.*

As down the glen one Easter morn
To a city fair rode I,
There Ireland's lines of marching men
In squadrons passed me by.

No pipes did hum and no battle drum
Did sound its dread tattoo,
But the Angeles bell o'er the Liffey swell
Rang out in the foggy dew.

Ride proudly high over Dublin town
We hung out the flag of war.
For 'twas better to die 'neath an Irish sky
Than at Suvla, Sud-el-bar.

And from the plains of Royal Meath
Strong men came hurrying through.
While Brittania's sons with their long-range guns
Sailed in by the foggy dew.

It was England bad o'er wild geese swore
That small nations might be free
But their lonely graves are by Suvla's waves
And the fringe of the grey north sea.

Oh had they died by Pearse's side
Or fought with Valera true
Their graves we'd keep where the Fenians sleep
'Neath the hills of the foggy dew.

The bravest fell as the sullen bell
Rang mournfully and clear
For those who died that Eastertide
In the springing of the year.

And the world did gaze in deep amaze
At those fearless men and true,
Who bore the fight that freedom's light
Might shine through the foggy dew.

'Foggy Dew', Jimmy Makem on *Tradition* recordings (1997).

DOCUMENT 18   **YEATS ON THE EASTER RISING**

*The poet W.B. Yeats had been a key influence during the 1890s Gaelic
Revival, a leading light in the New Literary Society and the Abbey Theatre,
where in 1902 his most nationalistic play,* Cathleen ni Houlihan, *was first
performed. Though he fell out with the Irish-Ireland movement, led by
Moran, he maintained contacts with Nationalist leaders. His initial reaction
to the Easter Rising is one of shock, if not despair, mingled with a fear for the
future and a respect for the bravery of the men involved.*

I have met them at close of day
Coming with vivid faces
From counter or desk among grey

Eighteenth-century houses.
I have passed with a nod of the head
Or polite meaningless words,
Or have lingered awhile and said
Polite meaningless words,
And thought before I had done
Of a mocking tale or a gibe
To please a companion
Around the fire at the club,
Being certain that they and I
But lived where motley is worn:
All changed, changed utterly:
A terrible beauty is born.

That woman's days were spent
In ignorant good-will,
Her nights in argument
Until her voice grew shrill.
What voice more sweet than hers
When, young and beautiful,
She rode to harriers?
This man had kept a school
And rode our winged horse;
This other his helper and friend
Was coming into his force;
He might have won fame in the end,
So sensitive his nature seemed,
So daring and sweet his thought.
This other man I had dreamed
A drunken, vainglorious lout.
He had done most bitter wrong
To some who are near my heart,
Yet I number him in the song;
He, too, has resigned his part
In the casual comedy;
He, too, has been changed in his turn,
Transformed utterly:
A terrible beauty is born.

Hearts with one purpose alone
Through summer and winter seem
Enchanted to a stone
To trouble the living stream.
The horse that comes from the road,
The rider, the birds that range
From cloud to tumbling cloud,

Minute by minute they change;
A shadow of cloud on the stream
Changes minute by minute;
A horse-hoof slides on the brim,
And a horse plashes within it;
The long-legged moor-hens dive,
And hens to moor-cocks call;
Minute by minute they live:
The stone's in the midst of all.

Too long a sacrifice
Can make a stone of the heart.
O when may it suffice?
That is Heaven's part, our part
To murmur name upon name,
As a mother names her child
When sleep at last has come
On limbs that had run wild.
What is it but nightfall?
No, no, not night but death;
Was it needless death after all?
For England may keep faith
For all that is done and said.
We know their dream; enough
To know they dreamed, and are dead;
And what if excess of love
Bewildered them till they died?
I write it out in a verse –
MacDonagh and MacBride
And Connolly and Pearse
Now and in time to be,
Wherever green is worn,
Are changed, changed utterly:
A terrible beauty is born.

'Easter 1916', *W.B. Yeats: Selected Poetry* (Penguin, London, 1991), pp. 119–21.

DOCUMENT 19   EYEWITNESS TO THE EASTER RISING

On Monday 24 April 1916 the Volunteers seized various buildings across Dublin and held them, against intense British bombardment, until their surrender on 29 April. The initial reaction of ordinary Dubliners was one of bemusement and hostility, though mixed in with a grudging respect for the bravery and even nobility of the insurgents. The extract is taken from an eye-

witness account written as events unfolded, and thus reflects immediate reactions and their gradual change. Stephens was a poet and writer, a supporter of Griffith and Sinn Féin.

Monday 24 April,

For an hour I tramped the city, seeing everywhere these knots of watchful strangers speaking together in low tones, and it sank into my mind that what I had heard was true, and that the City was in insurrection. It had been promised for so long, and had been threatened for so long. Now it was here. I had seen it in the Green, others had seen it in other parts – the same men clad in dark green and equipped with rifle, bayonet, and bandolier, the same silent activity. The police had disappeared from the streets. At that hour I did not see one policeman, nor did I see one for many days, and men said that several of them had been shot earlier in the morning; that an officer had been shot on the Portobello Bridge, that many soldiers had been killed, and that a good many civilians were dead also.

Around me as I walked the rumour of war and death was in the air. Continually and from every direction rifles were crackling and rolling; sometimes there was only one shot, again it would be a roll of firing crested with single, short explosions, and sinking again to whip-like snaps and whip-like echoes; then for a moment silence, and then again the guns leaped in the air. The rumour of positions, bridges, public places, railway stations, Government offices, having been seized was persistent, and was not denied by any voice. ...

Just then a man stepped on the footpath and walked directly to the barricade. He stopped and gripped the shafts of a lorry lodged near the centre. At that instant the Park exploded into life and sound; from nowhere armed men appeared at the railings, and they all shouted at the man.

'Put down that lorry. Get out and go away. Get out at once.'

'He is the man that owns the lorry,' said a voice beside me.

Dead silence fell on the people around while the man slowly drew his cart down by the footpath. Then three shots rang out in succession. At the distance he could not be missed, and it was obvious they were trying to frighten him. He dropped the shafts, and instead of going away he walked over to the Volunteers.

'He has a nerve,' said another voice behind me.

The man walked directly towards the Volunteers, who, to the number of about ten, were lining the railings. He walked slowly, bent a little forward, with one hand raised and one finger up as though he were going to make a speech. Ten guns were pointing at him, and a voice repeated many times:

'Go and put back that lorry or you are a dead man. Go before I count to four. One, two, three, four ... '

A rifle spat at him, and in two undulating movements the man sank on himself and sagged to the ground.

I ran to him with some other, while a woman screamed unmeaningly, all on one strident note. The man was picked up and carried to a hospital beside the Arts Club. There was a hole in the top of his head, and one does not know how ugly blood can look until it has been seen clotted in hair. As the poor man was being carried in, a woman plumped to her knees in the road and began not to scream but to screech.

At that moment the Volunteers were hated. The men by whom I was and who were lifting the body, roared into the railings :-

'We'll be coming back for you, damn you.'

From the railings there came no reply, and in an instant the place was again desert and silent, and the little green vistas were slumbering among the trees.

Thursday 27 April,

I met D.H. His chief emotion is one of astonishment at the organising powers displayed by the Volunteers. We have exchanged rumours, and found that our equipment in this direction is almost identical. He says Sheehy-Skeffington has been killed. That he was arrested in a house wherein arms were found, and was shot out of hand.

I hope this is another rumour, for, so far as my knowledge of him goes, he was not with the Volunteers, and it is said that he was antagonistic to the forcible methods for which the Volunteers stood. But the tale of his death is so persistent that one is inclined to believe it. ...

Later on this day I met Mrs. Sheehy-Skeffington in the street. She confirmed the rumour that her husband had been arrested on the previous day, but further than that she had no news. So far as I know the sole crime of which her husband had been guilty was that he called for a meeting of the citizens to enrol special constables and prevent looting.

Among the rumours it was stated with every accent of certitude that Madame Markievicz had been captured in George's Street, and taken to the Castle. It was also current that Sir Roger Casement had been captured at sea and had already been shot in the Tower of London. The names of several Volunteer Leaders are mentioned as being dead. But the surmise that steals timidly from one mouth flies boldly as a certitude from every mouth that repeats it, and truth itself would now be listened to with only a gossip's ear, but no person would believe a word of it.

This night also was calm and beautiful, but this night was the most sinister and woeful of those that have passed. The sound of artillery, of rifles, machine guns, grenades, did not cease even for a moment. From my window I saw a red flare that crept to the sky, and stole over it and remained there glaring; the smoke reached from the ground to the clouds, and I could see great red sparks go soaring to enormous heights; while always, in the calm air, hour after hour there was the buzzing and rattling and thudding of guns, and, but for the guns, silence.

James Stephens, *The Insurrection in Dublin* (Colin Smythe, London, 1916), pp. 13–17, 50–3.

DOCUMENT 20   THE MANSION HOUSE AGREEMENT, 1917

Though established in 1905, Sinn Féin did not become a serious political force until after the Easter Rising, when it began to recruit into its ranks many thousands of young, disillusioned Irishmen and women. Sinn Féin now embraced republicans, socialists, nationalists and even monarchists, a wide spectrum of opinion that necessitated a party meeting (ard-fheis) in October 1917 at the Mansion House in Dublin, to agree a form of words that provided the party with unity and a political objective. It pledged international recognition for an Irish republic in the first instance and once established then Ireland could choose her own system of government. The following extract comes from the conference and is an appeal by de Valera, the newly elected President of Sinn Féin, recommending the formula as a temporary but vital arrangement to allow them to concentrate on defeating the British.

The Constitution of this new movement which you have adopted is one which it may be well to lay stress on. It says that this organisation of Sinn Féin aims at securing international recognition for Ireland as an Independent Irish Republic. That is what I stand for, what I stood for in East Clare, and it is because I stand for that that I was elected here. I said in East Clare ... that I regarded that election as a monument to the dead. I regard my election here as a monument to the brave dead, and I believe that this is proof that they were right, that what they fought for – the complete and absolute freedom and separation from England – was the pious wish of every Irish heart. ... This Constitution that we are setting up says that we are striving to get international recognition for our Irish republic, and there is an added clause to it which I would like to explain, that, having achieved that status, the Irish people may by referendum freely choose their own forms of government. This is not the time for this, for this reason, that the only banner under which our freedom can be won at the present time is the republican banner. It is as an Irish Republic that we have a chance of getting international recognition. Some of us would wish, having got that recognition, to have a republican form of government. Some might have fault to find with that and prefer other forms of government. This is not the time for discussion on the best forms of government. But we are all united on this – that we want complete and absolute independence.

Speeches and Statements by Eamon de Valera 1917–73, ed. Maurice Moynihan (Gill & Macmillan, Dublin, 1980), pp. 6–8.

DOCUMENT 21   SINN FÉIN AND CONSCRIPTION, 1918

The British attempt to impose conscription onto Ireland met with near universal hostility. At the Mansion House on 18 April 1918, Sinn Féin brought together all political bodies in Ireland, including the Labour party, trades unions and the Irish Nationalist party, now under Dillon, to mount a campaign of resistance. The following declaration was passed at the meeting and provided the focus for a wave of agitations, that included a general strike. Against such a show of public sentiment the government backed down.

Taking our stand on Ireland's separate and distinct nationhood and affirming the principle of liberty that the governments of nations derive their just powers from the consent of the governed, we deny the right of the British Government, or any external authority, to impose compulsory service in Ireland against the clearly expressed will of the Irish people.

The passing of the Conscription bill by the British House of Commons must be regarded as a declaration of war on the Irish nation. The alternative to accepting it, as such, is to surrender our liberties and to acknowledge ourselves slaves.

It is in direct violation of the rights of small nationalities to self determination, which even the Prime Minister of England – now prepared to employ naked militarism to force this act upon Ireland – himself officially announced as an essential condition for peace at the Peace Conference.

The attempt to enforce it will be an unwarrantable aggression which we call upon all Irishmen to resist by the most effective means at their disposal.

Speeches and Statements by Eamon de Valera 1917–73, ed. Maurice Moynihan (Gill & Macmillan, Dublin, 1980), p. 13.

DOCUMENT 22   **TREATMENT OF A REPUBLICAN PRISONER**

The extract is taken from a statement given on 21 January by Timothy O'Connell, regarding his interrogation and treatment whilst in the custody of the British Auxiliary Forces. The Auxiliaries and the Black and Tans, who were recruited in Britain and arrived early in 1920, brought a new level of brutality into the policing of Ireland, which is reflected in the statement.

I was arrested on the morning of 2 January 1921 about a mile from the scene of the Kilmichael ambush. ... I was led to the guardroom where I had to take off all my clothes and was thoroughly searched. They found nothing ... so ... I was ordered to dress and taken to the back of the building where a hand-pump was shown to me. I was ordered to get to work turning this to supply the house with water. This job lasted non-stop for over an hour, and by then my palms were raw and bleeding. I was almost too weak to stand. It was now almost 24 hours since I had any food, or even a cup of tea ... I was brought back to the guardroom where I lay on the floor until about midnight when three Auxies came in and ordered me to my feet ... I was led into the room, and when about halfway through the room, the leader, a great big savage, suddenly turned round and before I could realise what was going to happen he lifted me off the floor with a punch. He didn't drop me, I kept on my feet and took at least a few more before I went down. I made no attempt to get up until one of the other two came at me with a bayonet ... Once again the savage moved in with a few more hay-makers, and put me down a second time. The blood was almost choking me by then: once more I was forced to stand up to face the puncher and take more punishment. Finally I went down to stay. I asked them to shoot me. The big fellow said 'no, we wouldn't have your blood on our hands', even though by then they had most of what I had on their hands and clothes as well as pools on the floor. ... My face had swollen to a lump of jelly, both my eyes were almost closed, and my nose was broken. I was brought some breakfast but I couldn't eat it as my teeth had gone right through my lips, and I couldn't open my mouth, save a small space in one corner. Through this small opening they fed me with soup, and it was almost a month before I could chew or swallow any solid food. ...

A few days after I was beaten up, I was taken before the big shots, Latimer, De Havilland and Sparrow, and questioned ... Next morning at the stroke of six I was brought before the big shots. Each had a gun in his hand. One stood behind me with a gun to my neck. They started with the usual questions whether I had made up my mind to give the information they wanted. I said I didn't have any to give. They kept at me for half an hour or so, but I refused to answer. One of them wanted to shoot me there and then, but was stopped by the others. ...

One Monday morning ... I was called out along with two other prisoners, the Barratt brothers of Coppeen. Three lorries were lined up each full of Auxies. We were ordered on board, one of us on each lorry, and were told that if one shot was fired at the lorries all three of us would be shot immediately.

'Statement by Timothy O'Connell, Ahaheera, Dunmanway, 21 January 1921', in A. O'Day and J. Stevenson (eds), *Irish Historical Documents since 1800* (Gill & Macmillan, Dublin, 1992), pp. 169–74.

DOCUMENT 23   **PROBLEMS FOR THE IRA**

Divisions within the Irish republican movement fell along several different fault-lines, politician versus man of action, moderate versus hardline republican, local activist versus central command. These strains foreshadowed later splits during the civil war, but for much of the period of the war of independence were subsumed by a common stance against the British. Dan Breen, from whose memoirs the extract is taken, was very much a man of action, responsible for the Soloheadbeg shootings in January 1919 and a leader of the IRA in Tipperary.

Our policy had been hitherto 'unofficial.' Dáil Eireann and General Headquarters of the I.R.A. had neither sanctioned it nor accepted the responsibility. Mick Collins promised to push our war policy in the 'proper quarters,' and it must be remembered that he was not only on the G.H.Q. staff but was also the Finance Minister.

Our war policy was not popular. Our G.H.Q. seemed to be lukewarm about it. The political wing certainly opposed it, and more than one T.D. privately denounced it. We succeeded in concealing our disagreements up to the time of the Truce. ...

At first the general public did not want the war. They seemed to forget that their vote at the general election led to the formal establishment of the Republic. Many were of the opinion that freedom could be won without any effort on their part. However, as the war progressed the vast majority of the people stood by us, and cheerfully took their share of the risks and hardships.

D. Breen, *My Fight for Irish Freedom* (Anvil, Dublin, 1981), pp. 102–3.

DOCUMENT 24   **TREATY NEGOTIATIONS, OCTOBER–**
                DECEMBER 1921

The delegation chosen to negotiate a treaty between Britain and Ireland consisted of Arthur Griffith, Michael Collins, Robert Barton, Gavan Duffy, Eamon Duggan and Erskine Childers. They were given full plenipotentiary powers by the Irish Cabinet, which implied the ability to bargain freely and sign the subsequent agreement. The Cabinet, however, accompanied these powers with a 'set of instructions' that limited the hand of the plenipotentiaries. Once the Treaty was signed on 6 December 1921, those hostile to it quoted these instructions as proof that the delegation had exceeded its brief.

7 October 1921 Credentials for team to negotiate 'envoys plenipotentiary'
(1) The plenipotentiaries have full powers as defined in their credentials.
(2) It is understood, however, that before decisions are finally reached on the main questions a dispatch notifying the intention of making these decisions will be sent to the members of the Cabinet in Dublin and that a reply will be awaited by the plenipotentiaries before the final decision is made.
(3) It is also understood that the complete text of the draft treaty about to be signed will be similarly submitted to Dublin and reply awaited.
(4) In case of break the text of final proposals from our side will be similarly submitted.
(5) It is understood that the Cabinet in Dublin will be kept regularly informed of the progress of negotiations.

Speeches and Statements by Eamon de Valera 1917–73, ed. Maurice Moynihan (Gill & Macmillan, Dublin, 1980), p. 55.

DOCUMENT 25   **ANGLO-IRISH TREATY, 1921**

The Treaty between Britain and Ireland was signed at 2.20 a.m. on 6 December after two gruelling months of intense negotiations. It established Ireland as a Dominion Free State, well beyond the Home Rule Bill which had been placed on the statute books in 1914. Though, with hindsight, it represented the limit to which a British government would be moved, many in Ireland saw it as a betrayal of the Irish Republic. On 7 January 1922 it was finally ratified in the Dáil by 64 votes to 57, a historic if slender margin that presaged the division of Ireland into pro- and anti-Treaty forces and civil war within a few months.

Articles Of Agreement For A Treaty Between Great Britain And Ireland, December 6, 1921

1. Ireland shall have the same Constitutional status in the community of Nations known as the British Empire as the Dominion of Canada, the Commonwealth of Australia, the Dominion of New Zealand, and the Union of South Africa, with a Parliament having powers to make laws for the peace, order, and good government of Ireland, and an Executive responsible to that Parliament, and shall be styled and known as the Irish Free State.

2. Subject to the provision hereinafter set out, the position of the Irish Free State in relation to the Imperial Parliament and Government and otherwise shall be that of the Dominion of Canada, and the law, practice, and Constitutional usage governing the relationship of the Crown or the representative of the Crown and of the Imperial Parliament to the Dominion of Canada shall govern their relationship to the Irish Free State.

3. The representative of the Crown in Ireland shall be appointed in like manner as the Governor-General of Canada, and in accordance with the practice observed in the making of such appointments.

4. The Oath to be taken by members of the Parliament of the Irish Free State shall be in the following form:-

I ... do solemnly swear true faith and allegiance to the Constitution of the Irish Free State as by law established, and that I will be faithful to H.M. King George V, his heirs and successors by law, in virtue of the common citizenship of Ireland with Great Britain and her adherence to and membership of the group of nations forming the British Commonwealth of Nations. ...

signed

on behalf of the Irish Delegation	on behalf of the British Delegation
Arthur Griffith	Lloyd George
Michael Collins	Austen Chamberlain
Robert Barton	Lord Birkenhead
Eamon Duggan	Winston Churchill
Gavan Duffy	L. Worthington Evans
	Hamar Greenwood

6 December 1921.

F. Pakenham, *Peace By Ordeal: The Negotiations of the Anglo-Irish Treaty 1921* (Jonathan Cape, London, 1935), pp. 288–92.

CHRONOLOGY

1494	Poynings' Law.
1541	Henry VIII takes title King of England and Ireland.
1610	Plantation of Ulster begins.
1690	June, William III lands in Ireland; July, Battle of the Boyne.
1695	Penal Laws limit Catholic rights.
1720	Declaratory Act.
1728	Franchise removed from Catholics.
1778	Catholic Relief Act allows landownership.
1782	May, Catholic Relief Act on education; June, Declaratory Act repealed – Grattan's Parliament (lasts until 1800).
1783	Renunciation Act.
1784	India Act.
1791	Canada Act.
1793	France declares war on Britain.
1796	French land in Ireland.
1798	May, rebellion in Ireland; June, Wexford Rebels defeated at Vinegar Hill; Sept., French land at Killala Bay; Nov., Wolfe Tone commits suicide in prison.
1800	Bill for Union between Britain and Ireland.
1801	Act of Union becomes law.
1813	Revival of Whiteboyism until 1818 (and again 1829–33).
1814	Peace Preservation Corps introduced in Ireland.
1817	British and Irish tax and exchequers fused.
1822	County constabulary created.
1823	Catholic Association formed.
1825	Free trade area around Britain and Ireland.
1828	O'Connell elected MP for Clare.

1829	Catholic emancipation.
1831	Elementary education for Ireland.
1832	Irish Tithe Composition Act.
1833	Irish Church Temporalities Act.
1835	Litchfield House Compact.
1838	Tithe-Rent Charge Act; July, Irish Poor Law.
1840	April, Loyal National Repeal Association founded; Aug., Irish Municipal Act.
1841	Peel's government (lasts until 1846).
1842	*The Nation* begins circulation.
1843	Oct., Clontarf meeting sees O'Connell's movement fold; Nov., Devon Commission on land established.
1844	Charitable Bequests Act.
1845	June, Maynooth Grant; Sept., reports of Famine (lasts until 1851).
1848	Attempted rising by Young Ireland.
1849	Encumbered Estates Act.
1850	Tenant League founded.
1858	Irish Republican Brotherhood (Fenians) formed.
1859	Mild depression (lasts until 1864)
1862	Funeral of Terence Bellew MacManus.
1865	Attempted Fenian rising.
1866	Fenian invasion of Canada.
1867	Feb., Fenians march on Chester Castle; Sept., Fenians ambush a prison van in Manchester; Nov., execution of three Fenian martyrs; Dec., Fenian bomb at Clerkenwell prison.
1868	Gladstone's first ministry; Aug., Amnesty Association formed.
1869	July, Irish Church Disestablishment Act; Nov., O'Donovan Rossa elected MP for Tipperary.
1870	May, Home Government association formed by Butt; Aug., Gladstone's first Land Act.
1873	March, Irish Universities Bill; Nov., Home Rule League formed.
1877	Aug., Parnell becomes President of the Home Rule Confederation.
1879	April, Land League formed; Oct., becomes the National Land League with Parnell elected President – New Departure.

1880	March, election returns Gladstone to government;
	May, Parnell chairman of the Irish Parliamentary Party;
	Sept., Ennis speech.
1881	March, Peace Preservation Act;
	Aug., Gladstone's second Land Act;
	Oct., Parnell arrested, calls for a 'rent strike' and
	Land League suppressed.
1882	May, Kilmainham 'treaty', Parnell released,
	Phoenix Park murders;
	Oct., Irish National League formed.
1883	Fenian outrages in Britain (continue into 1884).
1884	GAA formed by M.Cussack;
	Oct., recognition of Parnell by Catholic Church.
1885	June, fall of Gladstone's ministry,
	Salisbury forms ministry;
	Aug., Ashbourne Land Act;
	Nov., election;
	Dec., Hawarden 'kite'.
1886	Jan., Salisbury's ministry falls and Gladstone forms
	his third ministry;
	April, Home Rule Bill introduced;
	June, defeat of Home Rule Bill on second reading;
	July, election at which Salisbury forms second ministry.
1887	Balfour appointed Irish Chief Secretary, extension of
	the Land Purchase scheme;
	Sept., Mitchelstown riot.
1890	Nov., Parnell cited as co-respondent by O'Shea;
	Dec., Parnell deselected as leader of the Nationalist
	party.
1891	Congested Districts Board created, further extension
	to the Land Purchase scheme;
	Oct., Parnell dies.
1892	Gladstone's fourth ministry;
	July, National Literary Society formed;
	Nov., Gaelic League founded by Hyde.
1893	Sept., second Home Rule Bill, rejected in the Lords.
1894	Gladstone retires, replaced by Rosebery; creation of
	the ITUC.
1895	Salisbury forms his third ministry, G. Balfour Chief
	Secretary.
1896	Connolly forms Irish Socialist Republican party.

1897	People's Rights Association formed; extension to the Land Purchase scheme.
1898	William O'Brien forms the United Irish League; formation of the Abbey theatre.
1900	Nationalist party re-united; Salisbury's fourth ministry.
1902	Balfour replaces Salisbury as Unionist Prime Minister; Dec., Land Conference.
1903	Independent Orange Order formed by T.H. Sloan; Aug., Wyndham's Land Act.
1904	Dunraven forms Irish Reform Association.
1905	March, the UUC is formed; Sinn Féin formed by Griffiths; Dec., election lost by Unionists.
1906	Liberal government under Campbell-Bannerman (1908 Asquith).
1907	Irish Council's Bill is defeated; Playboy riots in Dublin.
1908	Strikes in Dublin docks; *Ne Temere* decree.
1910	Jan., general election; Feb., Carson leader of the Irish Unionists; Dec., general election.
1911	Aug., Parliament Act; *Motu Proprio* decree; Sept., Craigavon meeting; Nov., Bonar Law leader of the Tory party.
1912	April, 3rd Home Rule Bill; July, Blenheim Palace speech.
1913	UVF formed; March, League for Support of Ulster; Aug., Dublin lock-out; Sept., Provisional Government authorised by the UUC; Nov., Irish Volunteers formed.
1914	March, Asquith's offer of 'veiled' exclusion to Ulster: March, Curragh incident; April, gun running at Larne; July, Bachelors Walk incident; July, Buckingham Palace conference; Aug., Britain enters the war; Sept., Redmond promises Volunteers will fight wherever the Empire needs them and splits Volunteer movement.
1916	April, Easter Rising; July, failure of talks between Redmond, Carson and Lloyd George; Aug., Casement hung;

	Dec., formation of the Lloyd George coalition and Carson enters government.
1917	Feb., Roscommon by-election; July, Irish Convention meets; Sept., Ashe dies on hunger strike; Oct., Mansion House meeting.
1918	April, conscription imposed on Ireland; Nov., general election returns 73 Sinn Féiners who abstain from Westminster.
1919	Jan., Dáil Eireann constituted; Feb., Irish Labour leaders sit at Berne; April, de Valera elected President of the Irish Republic; July, Sinn Féin 'proclaimed' in Tipperary; Aug., oath of allegiance to the Dáil: Sept., Dáil declared illegal.
1920	Spring, arrival of Auxiliaries and Black & Tans; Aug., Restoration of Order Act; Oct., MacSwiney dies of hunger strike; Nov., Bloody Sunday; Dec., Government of Ireland Act partitions Ireland.
1921	May, attack on the Custom House; July, truce between Sinn Féin and Britain; Oct., negotiations open in London between Irish delegation and British government; Dec., Anglo-Irish Treaty repeals the Act of Union.

GLOSSARY

Agrarian crime Irish society, for much of this period, suffered from agrarian crime, often carried out through secret societies such as the Whiteboys or Oakboys. It was motivated by squabbles over landownership, tenancy, grazing rights, payment of tithes and rents, food prices, family or village disputes. It would operate according to communally understood 'conventions' that might well involve threats, the destruction of property, all the way through to violence against a person and even murder.

Ancient Order of Hibernians An avowedly sectarian organisation defending Catholic rights, which to some extent mirrored the Orange Order. It developed at a local level during the eighteenth century and was based in Ulster, where sectarian rivalries were at their most bitter. It grew rapidly in the 1880s and was of valuable electoral help to the Nationalist party.

Catholicism This was the religion of the majority of Irish people, mostly in the south and west of Ireland, and the source of British mistrust, for a Catholic's first loyalty was to Rome. Before the late eighteenth century Catholics suffered severe discrimination. These limits were eased by Parliament, most dramatically in 1829 when Catholics gained eligibility to sit at Westminster. Although Irish nationalism and Catholicism effected periodic cooperation, as under O'Connell and Parnell, it was not always an easy relationship. In particular the Catholic Church took a firm stance against Irish republicanism and IRA (and British) violence of the period 1916–21.

Clan na Gael An expatriate Irish revolutionary group founded in 1867 by Jerome Collins and based in the USA. Its most prominent and influential leader was John Devoy. The group had strong contacts with Fenianism and was an invaluable supply of money and men for activities back home. Indeed it was initiatives by Clan na Gael, in 1914, in opening talks with the German Ambassador that secured guns for the Irish cause and laid the groundwork for the Easter Rising.

Constitutionalism A commitment to political progress through established parliamentary channels and not through violence or 'physical force'.

Things, however, were not always as clear-cut. Parnell was wedded to constitutionalism but during the New Departure gained valuable influence and power from the nationwide attack on landlordism.

Cumann na nGaedheal A group established by Arthur Griffith in 1900 to further the cause of Irish independence. It appealed to all Irishmen and women, irrespective of religion or class, and was a forerunner to Sinn Féin.

Federalism A system of government where specific powers are devolved to a local or regional or even national level of administration. The range of powers devolved can vary a great deal, incorporating on the one hand a structure little different from local government, through to a system little short of full independence. The idea became popular during the late nineteenth century as a means of marrying the seemingly unbridgeable claims for national self-determination and central Imperial control.

Fenianism The Fenian movement or Irish Republican Brotherhood (IRB) was formed in 1858 by James Stephens and dedicated to the overthrow of British rule and creation of an Irish republic. Its name came from Gaelic folk-lore to denote a warrior. Fenians were committed, according to their oath of loyalty, to 'doing all in [their] power to establish the independence of Ireland', a remit that certainly involved violence. Its most famous incidents included the events of 1867, the bombing campaign in Britain in 1883–84 and the Easter Rising, all of the leaders being members of the IRB.

Gaelic A language and culture dominant in Ireland before the English invasion of the twelfth century. Gaelic stories and myths were revived by the Young Ireland movement of the 1840s, while in the 1890s, with the creation of the Gaelic League and the Gaelic Athletic Association, Gaelic sports and language were revived. These represented attempts to re-create a sense of Irish uniqueness, so as to distinguish the 'true' Irish from the British, and thus challenge the latter's 'right' to rule Ireland. Its endeavours were not very successful, for even after 1921 and despite the best efforts of the Irish government, English stubbornly remains the dominant language of Ireland.

Home Rule This gained widespread support from 1870 onwards, with the formation of the Home Government Association, which evolved into the Irish Nationalist party whose central policy was Home Rule for Ireland. Home Rule was the demand that Ireland should control her own affairs but remain within the British Empire, but was elastic enough to mean anything from the extension of local powers to full-blown independence from Britain. It was Parnell who converted Gladstone and the Liberal party to Home Rule in 1886, yet it had to wait another 30 years before it was placed on the statute book; and even then it was suspended for the duration of the war and finally abandoned.

Irish Citizen Army Formed by Connolly during the Dublin lock-out of 1913 to defend workers against the police. With its headquarters at Liberty Hall, it never attracted more than about 200–300 men and collapsed briefly before being revived in 1914. The Citizen Army played a leading role in the 1916 Rising, alongside the Volunteers.

Irish Volunteers Formed in November 1913 in response to the growth of the UVF and fears that the Liberal government would 'backslide' or compromise on the Home Rule Bill, then just six months from implementation. The initiative came from Eoin MacNeill, a known moderate who envisaged a force along the lines of the eighteenth-century Volunteers. But active behind the scenes were the IRB and especially Bulmer Hobson, who realised here was a movement that could be turned to their advantage. By May 1914 some 75,000 had enrolled and four months later the figure stood at 170,000. In September 1914 the organisation split over Redmond's decision to pledge their support to the British Empire. The majority followed Redmond, while some 10,000 went with MacNeill and for a neutral stance. This 10,000 would rise in rebellion in 1916.

'Killing Home Rule with Kindness' A label used to describe the series of reforms pushed through by the Tory governments of Salisbury and Balfour, with the intention of undermining the Irish demand for Home Rule by satisfying their social and economic grievances. The term implies a certain programmatic wholeness which was lacking, many of the reforms being *ad hoc* responses or temporary political compromises by ministers very much at sea with Irish affairs.

Land nationalisation A belief that land should be 'recovered' from the landlords, who were seen as an alien, English group, and given to the tenant farmers, establishing a sort of peasant proprietorship. Such ideas were associated closely with James Fintan Lalor and, by the 1880s, with Henry George.

Land war Depression in Ireland from 1878 led to a rise in evictions, collapsing markets, rural unemployment, falling sales and indebtedness. Under the guidance of the Land League, founded in 1879 by Michael Davitt, a supporter of land nationalisation, the agitation was focused against the landlords with a campaign of social ostracism and the withholding of rent, known as the land war. The reality was not as dramatic. The Land League operated only in certain areas while Parnell's call for a rent-strike in 1881 had little impact. By late 1881 the League collapsed.

Liberal Unionism These were Liberals who split with Gladstone over Home Rule. Led by Lord Hartington and Joseph Chamberlain, 93 Liberal Unionists voted against the Home Rule Bill on its second reading in the House of Commons. The bill was defeated and at the subsequent general election 72 of their number were re-elected. They now formed the Unionist Alliance with the Tories, though they maintained a separate organisation in the country and Parliament, and did not enter Cabinet until 1895.

Michelstown 'massacre' In 1887 the new Tory Chief Secretary, Arthur Balfour, was determined to uphold law and order in Ireland by a 'thorough' implementation of the new Crimes Act that led to frequent reports of police over-reaction. One such occasion at Mitchelstown, County Cork in September 1887, saw policemen shooting on a crowd, killing three people. Interestingly, at the time the Counsel to the Attorney General of Ireland was Edward Carson.

National League Formed by Parnell in October 1882, in the wake of the collapse of the Land League. It provided him with a national organisation, firmly under his control, able to secure loyal parliamentary candidates and mobilise support throughout the country.

The Nation A newspaper begun in 1842 by the Young Irelanders Thomas Davies and Charles Gavin Duffy to spread their brand of inclusive nationalism.

Orange Order Formed during the late eighteenth century as an organisation to defend Protestant interests, and particularly strong in Ulster. Drawing its name from William of Orange who defeated James II at the Battle of the Boyne (1690), the Orange Order was vigorously anti-Catholic. It played a major role in mobilising the Protestants of Ulster against Home Rule and in the creation of a Northern Ireland State, from 1921.

People's Rights Association Formed by Tim Healy in 1897 to counter Dillon's domination of the National Federation. It was essentially a vehicle for his own self-advancement, but it did espouse a more localist, Catholic bias compared to the national, professional organisation of Dillon.

Protestant Ascendancy This describes the domination of Ireland's political, economic and social life by a small, landed, Protestant and Anglo-Irish elite. The class was initially hostile to Union with Britain but in the face of growing Catholic, democratic pressures saw Union as the means to defend its economic, political and religious power. During the nineteenth century its position was gradually undercut, from government reforms such as disestablishment of the Irish Church, the rise of a powerful Nationalist political party and periodic campaigns to transform the existing system of landownership.

Presbyterian Presbyterians formed about 10 per cent of the population of Ireland, though concentration in the province of Ulster gave them significant political and economic power. Their faith was evangelical, emotional, based upon a direct connection between an individual and God, and vigorously anti-Catholic, even though, like Catholics, they stood outside the Established Anglican Church and suffered discrimination during the eighteenth century. With the rise of Catholic, democratic pressures, from the early nineteenth century, they joined Anglicans in a Protestant Alliance, but never lost their distinctiveness which by the 1880s was strong enough to lay the cultural and religious basis for Ulster Unionism.

Republicanism Irish republicans believed in breaking the connection between Britain and Ireland, regarding the Irish people as the 'sovereign' power and not the British Crown. Only, therefore, an elected Irish government and Head of State had the 'authority' to rule over the Irish nation. To achieve this many republicans, from Tone through to Pearse and Connolly, were willing to use violent revolution. However, absolute faith in an Irish republic created inflexibility when the time came to negotiate and compromise with the British. For everything else, be it repeal of the Union, Home Rule or Dominionhood as achieved in 1921, fell short of what they could accept.

Sectarianism A term used to describe inter-communal discrimination and violence, based around cultural, linguistic or religious differences. It was a common feature of Irish society, predominantly between Protestants and Catholics, and was at its most bitter in Ulster where the two communities lived in close proximity to each other. Some of the worst sectarian violence occurred in the period 1920–23 in and around Belfast and Derry, and would flare up again after 1968 to ignite The Troubles.

Ulster Custom A set of conventions that gave tenants reasonable security of tenure, as long as the rent was paid, and allowed them to sell any improvements made to their holding. These were demanded by tenants elsewhere, through the Tenant Protection Societies and Tenant League, although they were not in fact so limited to Ulster or as beneficial as many thought. Because they were 'customs' they had little basis in law, thus landlords could ignore them if they so desired.

Unionism A political movement which emerged in the 1880s to embrace those interests and sections of society who rejected Home Rule and desired a continuation of the Act of Union. The movement included Irish Protestants, Ulster 'loyalists', British Tories and, after 1886, those Liberals who had broken with Gladstone. It drew support throughout Ireland, but as southern Irish Unionism declined in power and effectiveness, Unionism became more associated with Ulster Unionists.

BIBLIOGRAPHY

Place of publication is London unless otherwise stated.

COMPANIONS AND DOCUMENT COLLECTIONS

1   Buckland, P., *Irish Unionism, 1885–1923: A Documentary History*, H.M. Stationery Office, Belfast, 1973.
2   Connolly, S.J. (ed.), *The Oxford Companion to Irish History*, Oxford University Press, Oxford, 1998.
3   Curtis, E. and McDowell, R.B. (eds), *Irish Historical Documents, 1172 to 1922*, Methuen, 1968.
4   Dunne, S. (ed.), *The Ireland Anthology*, Gill & Macmillan, Dublin, 1997.
5   Hepburn, A.C., *The Conflict of Nationality in Modern Ireland*, Arnold, 1980.
6   Mitchell, A. and O'Snodaigh, P. (eds), *Irish Political Documents, 1869–1916*, Irish Academic Press, Dublin, 1989.
7   O'Day, A. and Stevenson, J. (eds), *Irish Historical Documents since 1800*, Gill & Macmillan, Dublin, 1992.
8   Newman, P.R., *Companion to Irish History: From the Submission of Tyrone to Partition, 1603–1921*, Facts on File, Dublin, 1991.
9   Walker, B.M., *Parliamentary Election Results in Ireland, 1801–1922*, Gill & Macmillan, Dublin, 1978.
10   Ward-Perkins, S. (ed.), *Writings on Irish History*, Irish Committee of Historical Sciences, Dublin, 1996.

GENERAL

11   Bardon, J., *A History of Ulster*, Longman, 1992.
12   Beckett, J.C., *The Making of Modern Ireland, 1603–1923*, Faber & Faber, 1966.
13   Beckett, J.C., *A Short History of Ireland*, Faber & Faber, 1979.
14   Boyce, D.G., *The Revolution in Ireland, 1879–1923*, Macmillan, 1988.
15   Boyce, D.G., *The Irish Question and British Politics, 1868–1986*, Macmillan, 1988.

16   Boyce, D.G., *Nineteenth-Century Ireland: The Search for Stability*, Gill & Macmillan, Dublin, 1990.

17   Boyce, D.G., *Ireland, 1828–1923: From Ascendacy to Democracy*, Blackwell, Oxford, 1992.

18   Collins, P. (ed.), *Nationalism and Unionism: Conflict in Ireland, 1885–1921*, Institute of Irish Studies, Belfast, 1994.

19   Cosgrove, A. and McCartney, D. (eds), *Studies in Irish History presented to R. Dudley Edwards*, Gill & Macmillan, Dublin, 1979.

20   English, R. and Walker, G. (eds), *Unionism in Modern Ireland: New Perspectives on Politics and Culture*, Macmillan, 1996.

21   Foster, R.F., *Modern Ireland, 1600–1972*, Penguin, 1988.

22   Foster, R.F., *The Oxford Illustrated History of Ireland*, Oxford University Press, Oxford, 1989.

23   Foster, R.F., *Paddy and Mr Punch: Connections in Irish and English History*, Penguin, 1993.

24   Hennessey, T., *A History of Northern Ireland, 1920–1996*, Routledge, 1997.

25   Hoppen, T.H., *Ireland Since 1800: Conflict and Conformity*, Longman, 1989.

26   Kee, R., *The Green Flag*, Vols II & III, Penguin, 1972.

27   Lyons, F.S.L., *Ireland Since the Famine*, Weidenfeld & Nicolson, 1971.

28   Lyons, F.S.L. and Hawkins, R.A.J. (eds), *Ireland under the Union: Varieties of Tension: Essays in Honour of T.W. Moody*, Oxford University Press, Oxford, 1980.

29   MacDonagh, O., *States of Mind: A Study of Anglo-Irish Conflict, 1780–1980*, Allen & Unwin, 1983.

30   Mansergh, N., *The Irish Question, 1841–1921*, G. Allen & Unwin, 1975.

31   Morton, G., *Home Rule and the Irish Question*, Longman, 1980.

32   O'Brien, C.C., *States of Ireland*, Hutchinson, 1972.

33   O'Brien, C.C., *Ancestral Voices: Religion and Nationalism in Ireland*, Poolbeg, Dublin, 1994.

34   O'Day, A. (ed.), *Reactions to Irish Nationalism, 1865–1914*, Hambledon, 1987.

35   Stewart, A.T.Q., *The Narrow Ground: The Roots of Conflict in Ulster*, Faber & Faber, 1977.

36   Townshend, C., *Political Violence in Ireland: Government and Resistance Since 1848*, Clarendon Press, Oxford, 1984.

37   Vaughan, W.E. (ed.), *A New History of Ireland, VI, Ireland under the Union, 1870–1921*, Clarendon Press, Oxford, 1996.

HISTORIOGRAPHY

38   Boyce, D.G., 'Brahmins and Carnivores: The Irish Historian in Great Britain', *Irish Historical Studies*, XXV, 99, 1987, pp. 225–35.

39   Boyce, D.G. and O'Day, A. (eds), *The Making of Modern Irish History: Revisionism and the Revisionist Controversy*, Routledge, 1996.
40   Bradshaw, B., 'Nationalism and Historical Scholarship in Modern Ireland', *Irish Historical Studies*, XXVI, 104, 1989, pp. 329–51.
41   Brady, C. (ed.), *Interpreting Irish History: The Debate on Historical Revisionism, 1938–1994*, Irish Academic Press, Dublin, 1994.
42   Curtin, N., '"Varieties of Irishness": Historical Revisionism, Irish Style', *Journal of British Studies*, 35, 1996, pp. 195–219.
43   Doherty, G., 'National Identity and the Study of Irish History', *English Historical Review*, CXI, 441, 1996, pp. 324–49.
44   Ellis, S.G., 'Historiographical Debate: Representations of the Past in Ireland: Whose Past and Whose Present?', *Irish Historical Studies*, XXVII, 108, 1991, pp. 289–308.
45   English, R., 'Defining the Nation: Recent Historiography and Irish Nationalism', *European Review of History*, 2, 2, 1995, pp. 193–200.
46   Fanning, R., 'The Great Enchantment: Uses and Abuses of Modern Irish History', in C. Brady (ed.), *Interpreting Irish History: The Debate on Historical Revisionism, 1938–1994*, Irish Academic Press, Dublin, 1994.
47   Foster, R.F., 'We are all Revisionists now', *Irish Review*, I, 1986, pp. 1–5.
48   Foster, R.F., 'History and the Irish Question', in R.F. Foster, *Paddy and Mr Punch: Connections in Irish and English History*, Penguin, 1993.
49   Garvin, T., 'The Return of History: Collective Myths and Modern Nationalisms', *Irish Review*, 9, 1990, pp. 16–30.
50   Heaney, S., 'The Sense of the Past', *History-Ireland*, 1, 4, 1993, pp. 33–7.
51   Kiberd, D., 'The Elephant of Revolutionary Forgetfulness', in M. Ni Dhonnchadha and T. Diorgan, *Revising the Rising*, Field Day, Dublin, 1991.
52   Laffan, M., 'Insular Attitudes: The Revisionists and their Critics', in M. Ni Dhonnchadha and T. Diorgan, *Revising the Rising*, Field Day, Dublin, 1991.
53   Moody, T., 'Irish History and Irish Mythology', in C. Brady (ed.), *Interpreting Irish History: The Debate on Historical Revisionism, 1938–1994*, Irish Academic Press, Dublin, 1994.
54   Walker, B., *Dancing to History's Tune: History, Myth and Politics in Ireland*, Institute of Irish Studies, Belfast, 1996.

NINETEENTH CENTURY BACKGROUND, 1800–1868

55   Archer, J.R., 'Necessary Ambiguity: Nationalism and Myth in Ireland', *Eire-Ireland*, XIX, 2, 1987, pp. 23–37.
56   Belchem, J., 'Republican Spirit and Military Science: The "Irish Brigade" and Irish-American Nationalism in 1848', *Irish Historical Studies*, XXIX, 113, 1994, pp. 44–64.

57 Bernstein, G.L., 'Liberals, the Irish Famine and the Role of the State', *Irish Historical Studies*, XXIX, 116, 1995, pp. 513–36.
58 Bew, P., *Land and the National Question in Ireland, 1852–82*, Humanities Press, New Jersey, 1979.
59 Boyce, D.G., *Nationalism in Ireland*, Routledge, 1991.
60 Bull, P., *Land, Politics and Nationalism: A Study of the Irish Land Question*, Gill & Macmillan, Dublin, 1996.
61 Chamberlain, M.E., *Pax Britannica: British Foreign Policy, 1789–1914*, Longman, 1988.
62 Clark, S. *Social Origins of the Irish Land War*, Princeton University Press, Princeton, 1979.
63 Clark, S. and Donnelly, J.S. (eds), *Irish Peasants: Violence and Political Unrest, 1780–1914*, Manchester University Press, Manchester, 1983.
64 Colley, L., *Britons: Forging the Nation, 1707–1837*, Yale, New Haven, 1992.
65 Comerford, R.V., 'Fenianism as Pastime: The Appeal of Fenianism in the Mid-1860s', *Irish Historical Studies*, 22, 1981, pp. 239–50.
66 Comerford, R.V., *The Fenians in Context: Irish Politics and Society, 1848–1882*, Wolfhound, Dublin, 1985.
67 Connolly, S.J., *Religion and Society in Nineteenth-Century Ireland*, Studies in Irish Economic and Social History, Dublin, 1985.
68 Crossman, V., 'Emergency Legislation and Agrarian Disorder in Ireland, 1821–41', *Irish Historical Studies*, XXVII, 108, 1991, pp. 309–23.
69 Crossman, V., *Politics, Law and Order in Nineteenth-Century Ireland*, Gill & Macmillan, Dublin 1996.
70 Curtis, L.P., 'Moral and Physical Force: The Language of Violence in Irish Nationalism', *Journal of British Studies*, 27, 1988, pp. 150–89.
71 Daly, M.E., *The Famine in Ireland*, Gill & Macmillan, Dublin, 1986.
72 Daly, M.E., 'Revisionism and Irish History: The Great Famine', in D.G. Boyce and A. O'Day (eds), *The Making of Modern Irish History: Revisionism and the Revisionist Controversy*, Routledge, 1996.
73 Davies, R., *The Young Ireland Movement*, Gill & Macmillan, Dublin, 1987.
74 Donnelly, J.S., 'The Terry Alt Movement, 1829–31', *History-Ireland*, 2, 4, 1994, pp. 30–5.
75 Elliot, M., 'Ireland and the French Revolution', in H.T. Dickinson, *Britain and the French Revolution, 1789–1815*, Macmillan, 1989.
76 Garvin, T., 'The Anatomy of a Nationalist Revolution: Ireland 1858–1928', *Comparative Studies in Society and History*, XXV, 1986, pp. 468– 501.
77 Garvin, T., *Nationalist Revolutionaries in Ireland 1858–1928*, Clarendon Press, Oxford, 1987.
78 Geary, L., 'Epidemic Diseases of the Great Famine', *History-Ireland*, 4, 1, 1996, pp. 27–32.

79   Gilley, S., 'The Catholic Church and Revolution in Nineteenth-Century Ireland', in Y. Alexander and A. O'Day (eds), *Terrorism in Ireland*, Methuen, 1984.

80   Gray, P., 'The Triumph of Dogma: Ideology and Famine Relief', *History-Ireland*, 3, 2, 1995, pp. 26–34.

81   Hoppen, K.T., *Elections, Politics and Society in Ireland, 1832 to 1885*, Oxford University Press, Oxford, 1984.

82   Joyce, T., 'The American Civil War and Irish Nationalism', *History-Ireland*, 4, 2, 1996, pp. 36–41.

83   Kendle, J., *Ireland and the Federal Solution: The Debate over the United Kingdom Constitution, 1870–1921*, McGill-Queen's, Montreal, 1989.

84   Kennedy, L., *Colonialism, Religion and Nationalism in Ireland*, Institute of Irish Studies, Belfast, 1996.

85   Kerr, D., *Peel, Priests and Politics: Sir Robert Peel's Administration and the Roman Catholic Church in Ireland, 1841–46*, Oxford University Press, Oxford, 1982.

86   Lee, J.J., 'The Ribbonmen', in T.D. Williams (ed.), *Secret Societies in Ireland*, Gill & Macmillan, Dublin, 1973.

87   Lee, J.J., *The Modernisation of Irish Society*, Gill & Macmillan, Dublin, 1973.

88   Lowe, W.J., 'The Irish Constabulary in the Great Famine', *History-Ireland*, 5, 4, 1997, pp. 32–37.

89   MacDonagh, O., *Ireland: The Union and its Aftermath*, G. Allen and Unwin, 1977.

90   MacDonagh, O., 'O'Connell and Repeal, 1840–5', in M. Bentley and J. Stevenson (eds), *High and Low Politics in Modern Britain: Ten Studies*, Clarendon Press, Oxford, 1983.

91   Mandle, W.F., 'The IRB and the Beginnings of the Gaelic Athletic Association', *Irish Historical Studies*, XX, 1977, pp. 418–38.

92   Moody, T.W., *Davitt and Irish Revolution, 1848–82*, Oxford University Press, Oxford, 1981.

93   Newsinger, J., *Fenianism in Mid-Victorian Britain*, Pluto, 1994.

94   O'Broin, L., *Revolutionary Underground: The Story of the Irish Republican Brotherhood, 1858–1924*, Gill & Macmillan, Dublin, 1976.

95   O'Grada, C., *Ireland Before and After the Famine: Explorations in Economic History, 1800–1925*, Manchester University Press, Manchester, 1988.

96   O'Grada, C., *Ireland: A New Economic History, 1780–1939*, Oxford University Press, Oxford, 1994.

97   O'Ferrall, F., *Catholic Emancipation: Daniel O'Connell and the Birth of Irish Democracy, 1820–30*, Gill & Macmillan, Dublin, 1985.

98   Owens, G., '"A Moral insurrection": Faction Fighters, Public Demonstrations and the O'Connellite Campaign, 1828', *Irish Historical Studies*, XXX, 120, 1997, pp. 513–41.

99   Robinson, M., 'Daniel O'Connell: A Tribute', *History-Ireland*, 5, 4, 1997, pp. 26–31.

100 Sloan, R., 'O'Connell's Liberal Rivals in 1843', *Irish Historical Studies*, XXX, 117, 1996, pp. 47–65.

101 Stewart, R., *The Foundation of the Conservative Party, 1830–1867*, Longman, 1978

102 Takagami, S., 'The Fenian Rising in Dublin, March 1867', *Irish Historical Studies*, XXIX, 115, 1995, pp. 340–62

103 Thornley, D., *Issac Butt and Home Rule*, Macgibbon & Kee, 1964.

104 Vaughan, W.E., *Landlords and Tenants in Ireland, 1848–1904*, Studies in Irish Economic and Social History, Dublin, 1984.

105 Vaughan, W.E., *Landlords and Tenants in Mid-Victorian Ireland*, Clarendon Press, Oxford, 1994.

106 Ward, A.J., *The Irish Constitutional Tradition: Responsible Government and Modern Ireland, 1782–1992*, Irish Academic Press, Dublin, 1994.

107 Williams, T.D. (ed.), *Secret Societies in Ireland*, Gill & Macmillan, Dublin, 1973.

108 Winstanley, M.J., *Ireland and the Land Question, 1800–1922*, Methuen, 1984.

109 Zastoupil, L., 'Moral Government: J.S. Mill on Ireland', *Historical Journal*, XXVI, 1983, pp. 707–17

GLADSTONE, PARNELL AND HOME RULE, 1868–1890

110 Adelman, P., *Gladstone, Disraeli and Later Victorian Politics*, Longman, 1970.

111 Buckland, P., *The Anglo-Irish and the New Ireland, 1885–1922*, Gill & Macmillan, Dublin, 1972.

112 Buckland, P., *Ulster Unionism and the Origins of Northern Ireland, 1886–1922*, Gill & Macmillan, Dublin, 1973.

113 Cooke, A.B. and Vincent, J., *The Governing Passion: Cabinet Government and Party Politics in Britain, 1885–6*, Harvester, Brighton, 1974.

114 Comerford, R.V., 'Issac Butt and the Home Rule Party, 1870–77', in W.E. Vaughan (ed.), *A New History of Ireland, VI, Ireland under the Union, 1870–1921*, Clarendon Press, Oxford, 1996.

115 Comerford, R.V., 'The Land War and the Politics of Distress, 1877–82', in W.E. Vaughan (ed.), *A New History of Ireland, VI, Ireland under the Union, 1870–1921*, Clarendon Press, Oxford, 1996.

116 Davis, P., 'The Liberal Unionist Party and the Irish Policy of Lord Salisbury's Government, 1886–1892', *Historical Journal*, XVIII, 1, 1975, pp. 85–104.

117 Deane, S., 'Land and Soil: A Territorial Rhetoric', *History-Ireland*, 2, 1, 1994, pp. 31–4.

118   Gibbon, P., *The Origins of Ulster Unionism: The Formation of Popular Protestant Politics and Ideology in Nineteenth Century Ireland*, Manchester University Press, Manchester, 1975.

119   Goodlad, G.D., 'The Liberal Party and Gladstone's Land Purchase Bill of 1886', *Historical Journal*, XXXII, 3, 1989, pp. 627–41.

120   Hammond, J.L., *Gladstone and the Irish Nation*, Longman, 1938.

121   Heyck, T.W., 'Home Rule, Radicalism and the Liberal Party, 1886–1895', *Journal of British Studies*, XIII, 1974, pp. 66–91.

122   Kee, R., *The Laurel and the Ivy: The Story of Charles Stewart Parnell and Irish Nationalism*, Penguin, 1993.

123   Kendle, J., *Ireland and the Federal Solution: The Debate over the United Kingdom Constitution, 1870–1921*, McGill-Queens, Montreal, 1989.

124   Jackson, A., *The Ulster Party: Irish Unionists in the House of Commons, 1884–1911*, Clarendon Press, Oxford, 1989.

125   Jenkins, T.A., *Gladstone, Whiggery and the Liberal Party, 1874–1886*, Oxford University Press, Oxford, 1988.

126   Jenkins, T.A., *The Liberal Ascendancy, 1830–1886*, Macmillan, 1994.

127   Jordan, D., 'John O'Connor Power, Charles Stewart Parnell and the Centralisation of Popular Politics in Ireland', *Irish Historical Studies*, XXV, 1987, pp. 46–66.

128   Jordan, D., 'Irish National League and the "Unwritten Law": Rural Protest and Nation-Building in Ireland, 1882–1890', *Past & Present*, 158, 1998, pp. 148–71.

129   Loughlin, J., *Gladstone, Home Rule and the Ulster Question, 1882–93*, Gill and Macmillan, Atlantic Highlands, N.J., 1986.

130   Lubenow, W.C., 'Irish Home Rule and the Great Separation in the Liberal Party of 1886: The Dimensions of Parliamentary Liberalism', *Victorian Studies*, 26, 2, 1983.

131   Lubenow, W.C., *Parliamentary Politics and the Home Rule Crisis: The British House of Commons in 1886*, Oxford University Press, Oxford, 1988.

132   Lyons, F.S.L., 'The Aftermath of Parnell, 1891–1903', in W.E. Vaughan (ed.), *A New History of Ireland, VI, Ireland under the Union, 1870–1921*, Clarendon Press, Oxford, 1996.

133   Marsh, P.T., *The Discipline of Popular Government: Lord Salisbury's Domestic Statecraft, 1881–1902*, Harvester, Brighton, 1978.

134   Maume, P., 'Parnell and the IRB Oath', *Irish Historical Studies*, XXIX, 115, 1995, pp. 363–70.

135   Miller, D.W., *Queen's Rebels: Ulster Loyalism in Historical Perspective*, Gill & Macmillan, Dublin, 1978.

136   Moran, G., 'James Daly and the Rise and Fall of the Land League in the West of Ireland', *Irish Historical Studies*, XXIX, 114, 1994, pp. 189–207.

137   Moran, G., 'Near Famine: The Crisis in the West of Ireland, 1879–82', *Irish Studies Review*, 18, 1997, pp. 14–21.

138 O'Brien, C.C., *Parnell and his Party, 1880–90*, Clarendon Press, Oxford, 1957.

139 O'Callaghan, M., 'Parnellism and Crime: Constructing a Conservative Strategy of Containment, 1887–91', in D. McCartney (ed.), *Parnell: The Politics of Power*, Wolfhound, Dublin, 1991.

140 O'Day, A., *Parnell and the First Home Rule Episode*, Gill & Macmillan, Dublin, 1986.

141 O'Day, A., *Irish Home Rule, 1867–1921*, Manchester University Press, Manchester, 1998.

142 Parry, J.P., *The Rise and Fall of Liberal Government in Victorian Britain*, Yale, New Haven, 1993.

143 Quinault, R.E., 'Lord Randolph Churchill and Home Rule', *Irish Historical Studies*, XXI, 84, 1979, pp. 377–403.

144 Shannon, R., *The Age of Disraeli, 1868–1881: The Rise of Tory Democracy*, Longman, 1992.

145 Shannon, R., *The Age of Salisbury, 1881–1902: Unionism and Empire*, Longman, 1996.

146 Smith, J., *The Taming of Democracy: The Conservative Party, 1880–1924*, University of Wales, Cardiff, 1997.

147 Sykes, A., *The Rise and Fall of British Liberalism, 1776–1988*, Longman, 1997.

148 Walker, B.M., 'The Irish Electorate, 1868–1915', *Irish Historical Studies*, XVII, 71, 1973, pp. 359–406.

149 Walker, B.M, 'The 1885 and 1886 General Elections: A Milestone in Irish History', in P. Collins (ed.), *Nationalism and Unionism: Conflict in Ireland, 1885–1921*, Institute of Irish Studies, Belfast, 1994.

150 Warren, A., 'Gladstone, Land and Social Reconstruction in Ireland, 1881–1887', *Parliamentary History*, II, 1983, pp. 153–73.

BRITAIN AND IRELAND, 1890–1910

151 Bew, P., *Conflict and Conciliation in Ireland, 1890–1910: Parnellites and Radical Agrarians*, Oxford University Press, Oxford, 1987.

152 Bull, P., 'Land and Politics, 1879–1903', in D.G. Boyce (ed.), *The Revolution in Ireland, 1879–1923*, Macmillan, 1988.

153 Bull, P., 'The Significance of the Nationalist Response to the Irish Land Act of 1903', *Irish Historical Studies*, XXVIII, 111, 1993, pp. 283–305.

154 Callanan, F., *The Parnell Split, 1890–91*, Cork University Press, Cork, 1992.

155 Curran, C.P., 'Griffith, MacNeill and Pearse', *Studies*, LV, 1966, pp. 21–8.

156 Curtis, L.P., *Coercion and Conciliation in Ireland, 1880–1892*, Princeton University Press, Princeton, 1963.

157 D'Arcy, F., 'Irish Trade Unions before Congress', *History-Ireland*, 2, 2, 1994, pp. 25–30.

158　Gailey, A., 'Unionist Rhetoric and Irish Local Government Reform, 1895–1899', *Irish Historical Studies*, XXIV, 93, 1984, pp. 52–68.

159　Gailey, A., *Ireland and the Death of Kindness: The Experience of Constructive Unionism, 1890–1905*, Cork University Press, Cork, 1987.

160　Garvin, T., 'Priests and Patriots: Irish Separatism and the Fear of the Modern, 1890–1914', *Irish Historical Studies*, XXV, 97, 1986, pp. 67–81.

161　Hutchinson, J., *The Dynamics of Cultural Nationalism: The Gaelic Revival and the Creation of the Irish Nation State*, Macmillan, 1987.

162　Hutchinson, J., 'Irish Nationalism', in D.G. Boyce and A. O'Day (eds), *The Making of Modern Irish History: Revisionism and the Revisionist Controversy*, Routledge, 1996.

163　Jackson, A., 'Irish Unionism and the Russelite Threat', *Irish Historical Studies*, XXV, 100, 1987, pp. 376–404.

164　King, C. and Kennedy, L., 'Irish Co-operatives, 1894–1994: From Creameries at the Crossroads to Multinationals', *History-Ireland*, 2, 4, 1994, pp. 36–41.

165　Lyons, F.S.L., *Culture and Anarchy in Ireland, 1890–1939*, Oxford University Press, Oxford, 1979.

166　Maguire, M., 'The Organisation and Activism of Dublin's Protestant Working Class, 1883–1935', *Irish Historical Studies*, XXIX, 113, 1994, pp. 65–87.

167　Mitchell, A., *Labour in Irish Politics, 1890–1930: The Irish Labour Movement in an Age of Revolution*, Gill & Macmillan, Dublin, 1974.

168　O'Callaghan, M., *British High Politics and a Nationalist Ireland: Criminality, Land and the Law under Forster and Balfour*, Cork University Press, Cork, 1994.

169　O'Halpin, E., *The Decline of the Union: British Government in Ireland, 1892–1920*, Syracuse University Press, Syracuse, N.Y., 1987.

170　Shannon, C., *Arthur J. Balfour and Ireland, 1874–1922*, Catholic University Press, Washington, 1988.

171　Warwick-Haller, S., *William O'Brien and the Irish Land War*, Irish Academic Press, Dublin, 1990.

THE ULSTER CRISIS AND EASTER RISING, 1910–1916

172　Beckett, I.F.W., *The Army and the Curragh Incident*, Bodley Head, 1986.

173　Bew, P., *Ideology and the Irish Question: Ulster Unionism and Irish Nationalism, 1912–1916*, Clarendon Press, Oxford, 1994.

174　Boyce, D.G., 'Ireland and the First World War', *History-Ireland*, 2, 3, 1994, pp. 48–52.

175　Bhreathnach-Lynch, S., 'The Easter Rising 1916: Constructing a Canon in Art & Artefacts', *History-Ireland*, 5, 1, 1997, pp. 37–42.

176　Caulfield, M., *The Easter Rebellion*, Gill & Macmillan, Dublin, 1963.

177 Deane, S., 'Wherever Green is Read', in M. Ni Dhonnchadha and T. Dorgan (eds), *Revising the Rising*, Field Day, Dublin, 1991.

178 De Rossa, P., *Rebels: The Irish Rising of 1916*, Doubleday, New York, 1990.

179 Denman, T., ' "The Red Livery of Shame": The Campaign Against Army Recruitment in Ireland, 1899–1914', *Irish Historical Studies*, XXIX, 114, 1994, pp. 208–33.

180 Fergusson, J., *The Curragh Incident*, Faber & Faber, 1964.

181 Fitzpatrick, D., *The Two Islands, 1912–1939*, Oxford University Press, Oxford, 1998.

182 Foy, M., 'Ulster Unionist Propaganda against Home Rule, 1912–14', *History-Ireland*, 4, 1, 1996, pp. 49–53.

183 Gailey, A., 'King Carson: An Essay on the Invention of Leadership', *Irish Historical Studies*, XXX, 117, 1996, pp. 66–87.

184 Garvin, T., 'The Rising and Irish Democracy', in M. Ni Dhonnchadha and T. Dorgan (eds), *Revising the Rising*, Field Day, Dublin, 1991, pp. 21–8.

185 Greaves, C.D., *1916 As History: The Myth of the Blood Sacrifice*, Fulcrum Press, Dublin, 1991.

186 Hennessey T., *Dividing Ireland: World War 1 and Partition*, Routledge, 1998.

187 Jackson, A., 'Unionist Myths, 1912–1985', *Past & Present*, 136, 1992, pp. 164–81.

188 Jalland, P., 'United Kingdom Devolution 1910–14: Political Panacea or Tactical Diversion?', *English Historical Review*, 94, 373, 1979, pp. 757–85.

189 Jalland, P., *The Liberals and Ireland: The Ulster Question in British Politics to 1914*, Harvester, Brighton, 1980.

190 Kiberd, D., 'The Elephant of Revolutionary Forgetfulness', in M. Ni Dhonnchadha and T. Dorgan, (eds), *Revising the Rising*, Field Day, Dublin, 1991.

191 Laffan, M., *The Partition of Ireland, 1911–1925*, Dundalgen, Dundalk, 1983.

192 Lee, J.J., *Ireland, 1912–1985*, Cambridge University Press, Cambridge, 1989.

193 Longely, E., 'The Rising, the Somme and Irish Memory', in M. Ni Dhonnchadha and T. Dorgan (eds), *Revising the Rising*, Field Day, Dublin, 1991, pp. 29–49.

194 Mansergh, N., *The Unresolved Question: The Anglo-Irish Settlement and its Undoing, 1912–1972*, Yale, New Haven, 1991.

195 Martin, F.X., 'Origins of the Irish Rising', in D. Williams (ed.), *The Irish Struggle, 1916–1926*, Routledge, 1966.

196 Martin, F.X., *Leaders and Men of the Easter Rising: Dublin 1916*, Cornell University Press, New York, 1967.

197 Martin, F.X., '1916 – Myth, Fact, and Mystery', *Studia Hibernica*, 7, 1967, pp. 7–126.

198   Martin, F.X., 'The 1916 Rising – A Coup d'Etat or a "Bloody Protest"?', *Studia Hibernica*, 8, 1968, pp. 106–37.

199   Ni Dhonnchadha, M. and Dorgan, T. (eds), *Revising the Rising*, Field Day, Dublin, 1991.

200   O'Broin, L., *Dublin Castle and the 1916 Rising*, Sidgwick & Jackson, 1966.

201   Rodner, W.S., 'Leaguers, Covenanters, Moderates: British Support for Ulster, 1913–14', *Eire-Ireland*, 17, 13, 1982, pp. 68–85.

202   Smith, J., 'Bluff, Bluster and Brinkmanship: Andrew Bonar Law and the Third Home Rule Bill', *Historical Journal*, 36, 1, 1993, pp. 161–78.

203   Smith, J., 'Paralysing the Arm: Unionists and the Annual Army Act, 1911–1914', *Parliamentary History*, 15, 2, 1996, pp. 191–207.

204   Smith, J., 'Conservative Ideology and Representations of the Union with Ireland, 1885–1914', in M. Francis and I. Zweiniger-Bargielowska (eds), *The Conservatives and British Society, 1880–1980*, University of Wales, Cardiff, 1996.

205   Stewart, A.T.Q., *The Ulster Crisis: Resistance to Home Rule, 1912–1914*, Faber & Faber, 1967.

206   Townshend, C., 'The Suppression of the Easter Rising', *Bullan*, 1, 1, 1994, pp. 27–47.

BRITAIN AND IRELAND IN WAR AND REVOLUTION, 1916–1922.

207   Augusteijn, A., 'The Importance of Being Irish: Ideas and the Volunteers in Mayo and Tipperary', in D. Fitzpatrick (ed.), *Revolution? Ireland, 1917–23*, Trinity History Workshop, Dublin, 1990.

208   Augusteijn, J., *From Public Defiance to Guerrilla Warfare: The Experience of Ordinary Volunteers in the Irish War of Independence, 1916–1921*, Irish Academic Press, Dublin, 1996.

209   Bew, P., 'Sinn Féin, Agrarian Radicalism and the War of Independence, 1919–1921', in D.G. Boyce (ed.), *The Revolution in Ireland, 1879–1923*, Macmillan, 1988.

210   Bew, P., 'The Real Importance of Sir Roger Casement', *History-Ireland*, 2, 2, 1994, p 42–45.

211   Bowden, T., 'The Irish Underground and the War of Independence, 1919–1921', *Journal of Contemporary History*, VIII, 2, 1973, pp. 3–24.

212   Boyce, D.G., *Englishmen and Irish Troubles: British Public Opinion and the Making of Irish Policy, 1918–22*, Macmillan, 1971.

213   Boyce, D.G., 'The Origins of Northern Ireland, 1914–1922', *Modern History Review*, Nov. 1995, pp. 21–2.

214   Buckland, P., 'Carson, Craig and the Partition of Ireland', in P.Collins (ed.), *Nationalism and Unionism: Conflict in Ireland, 1885–1921*, Institute of Irish Studies, Belfast, 1994.

215 Canning, P., *British Policy towards Ireland, 1921–41*, Oxford University Press, Oxford, 1985.

216 English, R., '"Paying no Heed to Public Clamour": Irish Republican Solipsism in the 1930s', *Irish Historical Studies*, XXVIII, 112, 1993, pp. 426–39.

217 English, R., *Radicals and the Republic: Socialist Republicanism in the Irish Free State, 1925–1937*, Clarendon Press, Oxford, 1994.

218 English, R., '"The Inborn Hate of Things English": Ernie O'Malley and the Irish Revolution, 1916–1923', *Past & Present*, 151, 1996, pp. 174–99.

219 Fair, J.D., *British Inter-Party Conferences: A Study of the Procedure of Conciliation in British Politics, 1867–1921*, Clarendon Press, Oxford, 1980.

220 Fitzpatrick, D., *Politics and Irish Life, 1913–1921: Provincial Experience of War and Revolution*, Gill & Macmillan, Dublin, 1977.

221 Fitzpatrick, D., 'The Geography of Irish Nationalism, 1910–1921', *Past & Present*, 78, 1978, pp. 113–44.

222 Fitzpatrick, D. (ed.), *Revolution? Ireland, 1917–23*, Trinity History Workshop, Dublin, 1990.

223 Flynn, K.H., 'Soloheadbeg: What Really Happened?', *History-Ireland*, 5, 1, 1997, pp. 43–6.

224 Garvin, T., *1922: The Birth of Irish Democracy*, Gill & Macmillan, Dublin, 1996.

225 Harkness, D., *The Restless Dominion: The Irish Free State and the British Commonwealth of Nations, 1921–31*, New York University Press, New York, 1970.

226 Hart, P., 'Michael Collins and the Assassination of Sir Henry Wilson', *Irish Historical Studies*, XXVIII, 110, 1992, pp. 150–70.

227 Hart, P., *The I.R.A. and its Enemies: Violence and Community in Cork, 1916–1923*, Clarendon Press, Oxford, 1998.

228 Hopkinson, M., *Green Against Green: The Irish Civil War*, Gill & Macmillan, Dublin, 1988.

229 Hopkinson, M., 'Review Article: Biography of the Revolutionary Period: Michael Collins and Kevin Barry', *Irish Historical Studies*, XXVIII, 111, 1993, pp. 310–16.

230 Kostick, C., *Revolution in Ireland: Popular Militancy 1917 to 1923*, Pluto, 1996.

231 Kotsonouris, M., 'Revolutionary Justice – the Dáil Eireann Courts', *History-Ireland*, 2, 3, 1994, pp. 32–6.

232 Lawlor, S., *Britain and Ireland, 1914–23*, Gill & Macmillan, Dublin, 1983.

233 Lyons, F.S.L., 'The New Nationalism, 1916–1918', in W.E. Vaughan (ed.), *A New History of Ireland, VI, Ireland under the Union, 1870–1921*, Clarendon Press, Oxford, 1996.

234 Lyons, F.S.L., 'The War of Independence, 1919–21', in W.E. Vaughan (ed.), *A New History of Ireland, VI, Ireland under the Union, 1870–1921*, Clarendon Press, Oxford, 1996.

235 Mitchell, A., *Revolutionary Government: Dáil Eireann, 1919–22*, Gill & Macmillan, Dublin, 1995.

236 Morgan, K.O., *Consensus and Disunity: The Lloyd George Coalition Government, 1918–1922*, Clarendon Press, Oxford, 1979.

237 Murphy, B., 'The First Dáil Eireann', *History-Ireland*, 2, 1, 1994, pp. 41–6.

238 O'Brien, G., 'The Record of the First Dáil Debates', *Irish Historical Studies*, XXVIII, 111, 1993, pp. 306–10.

239 O'Connor Lysaght, R., 'A Saorstat is Born: How the Irish Free State Came into Being', in S. Hutton and P. Stewart (eds), *Ireland's Histories: Aspects of State, Society and Ideology*, Routledge, 1991, pp. 36–51.

240 O'Tuathaigh, G., 'Nationalist Ireland, 1912–1922: Aspects of Continuity and Change', in P. Collins (ed.), *Nationalism and Unionism: Conflict in Ireland, 1885–1921*, Institute of Irish Studies, Belfast, 1994.

241 Pakenham, F., *Peace by Ordeal: The Negotiations of the Anglo-Irish Treaty, 1921*, Jonathan Cape, 1935.

242 Rafferty, O., 'The Catholic Church and Partition, 1918–22', *Irish Studies Review*, 20, 1997, pp. 12–16.

243 Regan, J.M., 'The Politics of Reaction: The Dynamics of Treatyite Government and Policy, 1922–33', *Irish Historical Studies*, XXX, 120, 1997, pp. 542–63.

244 Staunton, E., 'The Boundary Commission Debacle 1925: Aftermath and Implications', *History-Ireland*, 4, 2, 1996, pp. 42–5.

245 Staunton, E., 'Reassessing Michael Collins's Northern Policy', *Irish Studies Review*, 20, 1997, pp. 9–11.

246 Townshend, C., *The British Campaign in Ireland, 1919–1921*, Oxford University Press, Oxford, 1975.

247 Townshend, C., 'The Irish Republican Army and the Development of Guerrilla Warfare, 1916–21', *English Historical Review*, 94, 1979, pp. 318–44.

248 Ward, M., 'The League of Women Delegates and Sinn Féin 1917', *History-Ireland*, 4, 3, 1996, pp. 37–41.

249 Williams, D. (ed.), *The Irish Struggle, 1916–1926*, Routledge, 1966.

BIOGRAPHY

250 Anderson, W.K., *James Connolly and the Irish Left*, Irish Academic Press, Dublin, 1994.

251 Allen, K., *The Politics of James Connolly*, Pluto, 1990.

252 Bew, P., *C.S. Parnell*, Gill & Macmillan, Dublin, 1980.

253 Bew, P., *John Redmond*, Gill & Macmillan, Dublin, 1996.

254 Blake, R., *The Unknown Prime Minister: The Life and Times of Andrew Bonar Law, 1858–1923*, Eyre & Spottiswoode, 1955.
255 Birkenhead, Earl of, *FE: F.E. Smith, 1st Earl of Birkenhead*, Eyre & Spottiswoode, 1965.
256 Bowman, J., *De Valera and the Ulster Qustion, 1917–1973*, Oxford University Press, Oxford, 1982.
257 Boyce, D.G. and O'Day, A. (eds), *Parnell in Perspective*, Routledge, 1991.
258 Buckland, P., *James Craig, Lord Craigavon*, Gill & Macmillan, Dublin, 1980.
259 Callanan, F., *T.M. Healy*, Cork University Press, Cork, 1996.
260 Charmley, J., *Churchill: The End of Glory*, Hodder & Stoughton, 1993.
261 Coogan, T.P., *Michael Collins: A Biography*, Arrow, 1991.
262 Davis, R., *Arthur Griffith*, Historical Association of Ireland, Dublin, 1976.
263 Edwards, R.D., *Patrick Pearse: The Triumph of Failure*, Faber & Faber, 1977.
264 Forester, M., *Michael Collins: The Lost Leader*, Sphere, 1971.
265 Hyde, H.M., *Carson*, Heinemann, 1953.
266 Hyland, J.L., *James Connolly*, Historical Association of Ireland, Dublin, 1996.
267 Jackson, A., *Sir Edward Carson*, Historical Association of Ireland, Dublin, 1993.
268 Jenkins, R., *Asquith*, Collins, 1964.
269 Jenkins, R., *Gladstone*, Macmillan, 1995.
270 Kendle, J., *Walter Long, Ireland and the Union, 1905–1920*, McGill-Queen's, Montreal, 1992.
271 Longford, Earl of and O'Neill, P., *Eamon de Valera*, Hutchinson, 1970.
272 Lyons, F.S.L., *John Dillon: A Biography*, Routledge, 1968.
273 Lyons, F.S.L., *Charles Stewart Parnell*, Collins, 1977.
274 Matthew, H.C.G., *Gladstone, 1809–1874*, Clarendon Press, Oxford, 1986.
275 Matthew, H.C.G., *Gladstone, 1875–1898*, Clarendon Press, Oxford, 1995.
276 Maume, P., *D.P. Moran*, Gill & Macmillan, Dublin, 1997.
277 McCartney, D. (ed.), *Parnell: The Politics of Power*, Wolfhound, Dublin, 1991.
278 Morgan, A., *James Connolly: A Political Biography*, Manchester University Press, Manchester, 1988.
279 O'Connor, F., *The Big Fellow: Michael Collins and the Irish Revolution*, Corgi, 1965.
280 O'Ferrall, *Daniel O'Connell*, Gill & Macmillan, Dublin, 1981.
281 Ryle Dwyer, T., *De Valera: The Man and his Myths*, Poolbeg, Dublin, 1991.

CULTURAL, POST-COLONIAL, WOMEN'S STUDIES

282 Anderson, B., *Imagined Communities: Reflections on the Origin and Spread of Nationalism*, Verso, 1983.

283 Brennan, H., 'Reinventing Tradition: The Boundaries of Irish Dance', *History-Ireland*, 2, 2, 1994, pp. 22–4.

284 Brett, D., *The Construction of Heritage*, Cork University Press, Cork, 1996.

285 Brown, T., 'Review Article: New Literary Histories', *Irish Historical Studies*, XXX, 119, 1997, pp. 462–70.

286 Cairns, D. and Richards, S., *Writing Ireland: Colonialism, Nationalism and Culture*, Manchester University Press, Manchester, 1988.

287 Connolly, S.J. (ed.), *Kingdom United? Great Britain and Ireland since 1500: Integration and Diversity*, Four Courts, Dublin, 1998.

288 Cullen, M., 'History Women and History Men: The Politics of Women's History', *History-Ireland*, 2, 2, 1994, pp. 31–6.

289 Curtin, C., Jackson, P. and O'Connor, B. (eds), *Gender in Irish Society*, Studies in Irish Society III, Galway, 1987.

290 Dalton, G., 'The Tradition of Blood Sacrifice to the Goddess Eire', *Studies*, LXIII, 1974.

291 Deane, S., *Strange Country: Modernity and Nationhood in Irish Writing Since 1790*, Clarendon Press, Oxford, 1997.

292 Finlayson, A., 'Nationalism as Ideological Interpellation: The Case of Ulster Loyalism', *Ethnic and Racial Studies*, 19, 1, 1996, pp. 88–111.

293 Fitzpatrick, D., 'Review Article: Women, Gender and the Writing of Irish History', *Irish Historical Studies*, XXVII, 107, 1991, pp. 267–73.

294 Foley, T. and Ryder, S. (eds), *Ideology and Ireland in the Nineteenth Century*, Four Courts, Dublin, 1998.

295 Gailey, A., 'The Nature of Tradition', *Folklore*, 100, 2, 1989, pp. 143–61.

296 Gibbons, L., 'Race Against Time: Racial Discourse and Irish History', *Oxford Literary Review*, 13, 1991, pp. 94–117.

297 Graham, B. (ed.), *In Search of Ireland: A Cultural Geography*, Routledge, 1997.

298 Hadfield, A. and McVeagh, J. (eds), *Strangers to That Land: British Perceptions of Ireland from the Reformation to the Famine*, Colin Smythe, 1994.

299 Hobsbawm, E. and Ranger, T. (eds), *The Invention of Tradition*, Cambridge University Press, Cambridge, 1983.

300 Kiberd, D., *Inventing Ireland*, Jonathan Cape, 1995.

301 Livesay, J. and Murray, S., 'Review Article: Post-colonial Theory and Modern Irish Culture', *Irish Historical Studies*, XXX, 119, 1997, pp. 452– 61.

302 O'Brien, E., 'The Epistemology of Nationalism', *Irish Studies Review*, 17, 1996/7, pp. 15–20.

303 Stewart, B., 'Inside Nationalism: A Meditation upon *Inventing Ireland*', *Irish Studies Review*, 6, 1, 1998, pp. 5–16.

304 Valente, J., 'The Myth of Sovereignty: Gender in the Literature of Irish Nationalism', *English Literary History*, 61, 1994, pp. 189–210.

305 Ward, M., *Unmanageable Revolutionaries: Women and Irish Nationalism*, Pluto, 1989.

306 Ward, M., 'Irish Women and Nationalism', *Irish Studies Review*, 17, 1996/7, pp. 8–14.

CONTEMPORARY WORKS, LETTERS AND DIARIES

307 Barry, T., *Guerrilla Days in Ireland*, Anvil, Dublin, 1949.

308 Breen, D., *My Fight for Irish Freedom*, Anvil, Dublin, 1964.

309 Brennan-Whitmore, W.J., *Dublin Burning: The Easter Rising from Behind the Barricades*, Gill & Macmillan, Dublin, 1996.

310 Collins, M., *The Path to Freedom*, Talbort, Dublin, 1922.

311 Kearney, P., *'My Dear Eva': Letters from Internment Camp, 1921*, Anvil, Dublin, 1976.

312 MacNeill, E., 'The North Began', *Sinn Féin Pamphlet*, 1914, in T. Hennessey, *Dividing Ireland: World War 1 and Partition*, Routledge, 1998.

313 Matthew, H.C.G., *The Gladstone Diaries with Cabinet Minutes and Prime-Ministerial Correspondence*, Vols IV–XIV, Oxford University Press, Oxford, 1968–94.

314 Middlemas, K. (ed.), *Thomas Jones Whitehall Diary: Volume III Ireland, 1918–1925*, Oxford University Press, Oxford, 1971.

315 Moynihan, M., *Speeches and Statements by Eamon de Valera, 1917–73*, Gill & Macmillan, Dublin, 1980.

316 O'Broin, L. (ed.), *In Great Haste: The Letters of Michael Collins and Kitty Kiernan*, Gill & Macmillan, Dublin, 1983.

317 Pearse, P., *Political Writings and Speeches*, Talbort, Dublin, 1966.

318 Stephens, J., *The Insurrection in Dublin*, Colin Smythe, 1916.

319 Vincent, J. (ed.), *The Later Derby Diaries: Home Rule, Liberal Unionism and Aristocratic Life in Late Victorian England*, University of Bristol, Bristol, 1981.

320 Wilson, T. (ed.), *The Political Diaries of C.P.Scott, 1911–1928*, Collins, 1970.

INDEX